WOMEN'S CAREER PATTERNS

Influences on Work Stability

Elizabeth Maret

UNIVERSITY
PRESS OF
AMERICA

LANHAM • NEW YORK • LONDON

SYNOPSIS

Current knowledge about the market work of women is predicated on very limited perceptions and research. In both the academic and popular literature, women tend to be typified as "secondary workers," propelled into the labor market as the result of pathological circumstances and needs. Yet, there is surprisingly little systematic knowledge about the causes or even the nature of women's lifelong market work patterns. Such limited knowledge is a deterrent to rational resource policies in both the private and public sectors.

An orientation toward women which recognizes (1) differences as well as similarities in work behavior and (2) positive as well as pathological reasons for market work is overdue in the literature. The present study seeks to expand knowledge about women's place in modern American society through a systematic analysis of the career patterns of 5,000 women. The study first documents differences in the worklife career patterns of women and then investigates individual (supply) and structural (demand) reasons for these differences. This has not been done elsewhere in the literature.

Another unique feature of the work is that it provides both historical overview and contemporary analysis of women's labor market involvement. The book is organized in two parts. Part One provides an historical background of trends in women's gainful employment and also summarizes differences observed between men and women. Part Two presents new empirical findings regarding influences on the career patterns of mature women.

The book reports the first systematic effort to document the nature and causes of women's life-long market work patterns. Based on data from the National Longitudinal Surveys of Work Experience (NLS data), the empirical analysis begins with the description of women's lifetime career patterns and then offers an assessment of the major influences on their work stability. The findings suggest a rich diversity in the market work experiences of contemporary women; they also illuminate the importance of individual and structural factors in explaining women's market stability.

This volume is the first of a two-part research

series on "Women and the American Occupational Structure," originally supported by small grants from the Manpower Administration of the U.S. Department of Labor (1974-1975) and from the College of Liberal Arts at Texas A&M University (1976-1977). This volume reports a conceptual refinement and empirical analysis of women's career patterns. Such analysis is of importance in its own right; it is also a necessary "first step" for subsequent analysis of women's status attainment and occupational mobility. The conclusions provided here are, of course, the sole responsibility of the author, and do not reflect any institutional endorsement. Some of the material in this volume has been published by the National Technical Information Service and the Bureau of Labor Statistics, U. S. Department of Labor.

Table of Contents

Table of Contents (cont.)

PREFACE

Housekeeping is still the main occupation of American women, but no longer the only occupation of most of them. More than half of all women between the ages of eighteen and fifty-five now spend at least part of each year working for pay (Robert W. Smuts, _Women and Work in America_, 1971:1).

Where is women's place? In the United States today, as in most urban-industrial societies, women constitute almost one-half of the labor force, and nine out of ten American women participate in the labor force at some point in their lives. On the other hand, women continue to provide most of the homemaking, childrearing, and other "volunteer" community services, which because they are unpaid are often forgotten in economic analysis, but without which no society could long endure. These facts are _not_ offered by way of an answer to the question of women's place in contemporary American society. They are offered in refutation of the question itself. Women in contemporary American society occupy no one place.

This report is concerned with the women who seek rewards from sustenance activities performed outside the home. It is concerned with their investments and attainments in an occupational structure defined by pursuits for pay or profit. Such an emphasis is justified by the statistical observations that follow. However, this study is not intended to legitimate the gross over-simplification that women's place is now in the labor force. Nor is it intended to legitimate the gross underestimation of women's contributions outside the labor force. Rather, the emphasis comes from the efforts to explore one neglected area of women's endeavors—an area which consists of a variety of places in the American occupational structure.

DATA

Data used to supplement the historical analysis presented in Part One, were taken from reports published by the U.S. Bureau of Census and the U.S. Department of Labor. Statistics on the labor force status and participation rates of women, used to compare the present findings regarding patterns of labor force attachment in Part Two, were taken primarily from Bowen and Finegan (1969). The major empirical analysis of mature American women reported in this book is based on data obtained from the U.S. Department of Labor's National Longitudinal Surveys of Work Experience (NLS data).

The National Longitudinal Surveys were commenced early in 1965 when the Office of Manpower Policy, Evaluation, and Research of the United States Department of Labor contracted with the Center for Human Resource Research at Ohio State University for longitudinal studies of the labor market experience of the non-institutionalized civilian population in the United States. Because of budget constraints, a representative sample of the total population was precluded, and four age-sex groupings of the population were selected for study on the grounds that each of these groupings faces special labor market problems of concern to policy makers.

For each group, a national probability sample of approximately 5,000 individuals was drawn by the U.S. Bureau of the Census from households in 235 sampling areas (those that constituted the primary sampling units in the experimental Monthly Labor Survey conducted between 1964 and late 1966), which represented every state and the District of Columbia. In order to ensure statistically reliable estimates for blacks, a sampling ratio three to four times as great as that for whites was used yielding samples of approximately 3,500 whites and 1,500 "non-Caucasians." The initial strategy of the NLS project called for annual interviews over a five-year period. In other words, there were to have been six interviews with each group. However, cost considerations dictated some revision in strategy.

The research makes use of the Ohio State cohort file on mature women; women who were 30 to 44 years of age at the time of the first survey in 1967. This file is comprised of responses to the 1967, 1969, and 1971 interviews and of responses to the brief mailed questionnaire used in 1968. There was, of course, some attrition between the 1967 and 1971 surveys, but sample shrinkage was remarkably small. Approximately 90 percent of the original sample of 5,083 women interviewed in 1967 were reinterviewed in 1971 (N=4,575).

Although the concern of the present study is not for the special problems of homemakers re-entering the labor force, the advantages for this research ensuing the NLS data on mature women far outweigh any limitations imposed by the secondary analysis. In general, the NLS data constitutes not only one of the most reliable but also one of the richest sources of information on the long-term labor market behavior of women in the United States.

The National Longitudinal Surveys of Work Experience provide a wealth of information about the labor market experiences of mature women in the United States. Data from these surveys yield measures of many dimensions of labor market activity and status. Information on time and duration of respondent's jobs provide a basis for analyzing longitudinal involvement in the labor force. Data on family background, education and training, condition of health, and characteristics of other members of the respondents' households are also available. Hence, NLS data provide information on variables that pertain to the social origins of respondents, such as the structure and status of their families of orientation, and information on recent and current aspects of respondents' situations that may directly or indirectly affect their recruitment and return in the American labor force.

Given the goal of this book to describe the major career experiences of American women, the temporal features of the National Longitudinal Surveys are particularly fortunate. Most important, the data for mature women permit the identification of life-cycle work patterns which are neither temporary nor capricious. In addition, these National Longitudinal Surveys of Work Experience offer an important potential for the continuing analysis of women in the American occupational structure. Surveys of the mature women cohort are now planned through 1983. The NLS young women cohort also offers the potential for analysis of women who are commencing careers in the American occupational structure.

P A R T   I

WOMEN IN THE AMERICAN LABOR FORCE:
An Historical Overview

Part One is concerned with the historical aspects of women's involvement in the American occupational structure as a background for the empirical analysis to follow in Part Two. By definition, the American occupational structure is limited to only certain positions; in particular, positions filled by members of the labor force. The American occupational structure does not include most jobs performed in the home or in unpaid services to families, communities, or society. In other words, the American occupational structure does not include many of the jobs traditionally performed by women. Questions concerning the extent of women's involvement in the American labor force are thus preliminary to many questions of concern about women's attainments in the occupational status structure.

Chapter One reviews secular trends in women's labor force participation and reviews previous findings pertaining to the characteristics of these "working women." Chapter Two highlights ways in which female labor force participation has tended, historically, to differ from that of males. These chapters of Part I present materials which are important for interpreting the new empirical findings reported in Part II. The reviews establish the need for investigating the lifetime supply of labor provided by women and they identify potential influences on their career patterns.

CHAPTER ONE

FEMALE LABOR FORCE PARTICIPATION

"10 Facts on Women Workers"

1. About 43 million women were in the labor force in 1979; they constituted more than two-fifths of all workers.

2. Sixty percent of all women 18 to 64--the usual working ages--were workers in 1979, compared with 88 percent of men. Fifty-one percent of all women 16 and over were workers. Labor force participation was highest among women 20 to 24.

3. Fifty-three percent of all black women were in the labor force in 1979 (5.0 million); they accounted for nearly half of all black workers.

4. Forty-seven percent of Spanish-origin women were in the labor force in March 1979 (2.0 million); they accounted for 39 percent of all Spanish-origin workers.

5. Women accounted for nearly three-fifths of the increase in the civilian labor force in the last decade--about 13 million women compared with more than 9 million men.

6. In 1977, the average woman could expect to spend 27.6 years of her life in the work force, compared with 38.3 years for men.

7. The more education a woman has the greater the likelihood she will seek paid employment. Among women with 4 or more years of college, about 2 out of 3 were in the labor force in 1979.

8. The average woman worker is as well educated as the average man worker; both have completed a median of 12.6 years of schooling.

9. The number of working mothers has increased more than tenfold since the period immediately preceding World War II, while the number of working women more than tripled. Fifty-five percent of all mothers with children under 18 years (16.6 million) were in the labor force in 1979; 45 percent of mothers with preschool children were working.

10. The 6.0 million working mothers with preschool children in 1979 had 7.2 million children under age 6, compared with 5.1 million working mothers with 6.1 million children under 6 years of age in 1974.

(U.S. Department of Labor, 1980)

> Women made up 43 percent of the U.S. labor force in 1980, up from 29 percent in 1950, and 52 percent of all women 16 and over were working or looking for work compared to 34 percent in 1950. The surge in women's employment is linked to more delayed marriage, divorce, and separation, women's increased education, lower fertility, rapid growth in clerical and service jobs, inflation, and changed attitudes toward "women's place." Employment has risen fastest among married women, especially married mothers of children under 6, 45 percent of whom are now in the labor force.
> (Linda J. Waite, 1981)

Although there remains considerable disagreement in the literature regarding trends in female labor force participation from the turn of the century to 1950,[1] there is no ambivalence regarding the trends since the 1940's--upward. Since the post World War II era, there has been a steady increase in the representation of women in the American labor force. Table 1.1 shows the increase in female representation from 1940 to 1980, in terms (a) of the female labor force participation rate and (b) of females as a percentage of the total labor force.

According to government figures, 44 million women were in the labor force in 1980. This figure exceeds the 1944 wartime employment peak by 24 million and the 1940 prewar figure by 30 million. Not all categories of women contributed equally to this tremendous growth. Between 1940 and 1980, the number of married women in the labor force rose most dramatically and the increased tendency of married women to enter the labor force has often been suggested as "the most important factor in the growth of the woman labor force" (Women's Bureau, 1969:23).

By March 1980, 25 million married women, half of all wives living with their husbands, were working or looking for work. These women made up 56 percent of the female labor force. But employment rates have gone up fastest among women with dependent age children, especially mothers of preschool children. Between 1950 and 1980, labor force participation rates for married

TABLE 1.1: THE GROWTH OF WOMANPOWER

Year	Women workers as percent of female population[1]	(Men)	Women Workers as percent of all workers[2]
1980	51.2	(77.2)	42.5
1975	46.3		39.9
1970	43.2		38.1
1965	38.3		35.0
1960	37.4		33.3
1955	34.8		31.2
1950	33.0	(86.4)	29.1
1945	38.1		36.1
1940	28.9		25.4

[1]Participation rates of women 16 years of age and over

[2]Civilian labor force

Source for 1940-1970; U.S. Department of Labor, Women's Bureau (1975:11)

for 1975-1980; U.S. Department of Labor, Bureau of Labor Statistics (1980:3)

8

mothers with children under six increased by almost 400 percent (from 12 to 45). By 1970, participation rates for women with children under 18 began to exceed those for married women without children. Currently, 56.6 percent of women with children under age 18 are working outside the home, compared to 48.0 percent of women with no children under 18. This total of 56.6 percent for women with dependent-age children includes 52 percent of never married women with children; 54 percent for women who are married with husband present; 60 percent for women who are married with husband absent; 59 percent of widowed women; and 78 percent of divorced women (Waite, 1981:22).

In part, the growth of womanpower can be accounted for by purely demographic phenomena, such as simple increases in the size of the female population and in the numbers of married women. However, the increase in participation rates for women and the disproportionate increases for some categories of women are not so simply explained. For example, the increase in the representation of married women from 1940 to 1967 constituted an increase of 276 percent; "an increase substantially larger than their 52 percent rise in the population" (Women's Bureau, 1969:24). These dramatic and disproportionate increases in women's entrance into the American labor force are said to be due to "a combination of demographic, economic, and social developments" (Women's Bureau, 1969:9).

Many systematic efforts to explain the long-run upward trend in the employment of women outside the home (see in particular, Bancroft, 1958; Bowen and Finegan, 1969; Durand, 1968 ed.; Long, 1958) have explored concomitant changes in several demographic variables such as (a) the sex-ratio, (b) age structure, (c) farm residence, (d) marital composition, and (e) fertility. Regarding the trend from 1940 to 1950, Bancroft (1958:43) notes that "vast shifts of population brought labor supply from farms into areas where demand for war workers very often carried over to the postwar years," and that such shifts tended to expand the labor force participation of women. Changes in the ratio of women to men in the population, during the war and subsequently, have also operated to increase the participation rates of women (see for example, McNally, 1968; Women's Bureau, 1969). However, Bancroft concludes (1958:87) such demographic changes can "account only in small part for the changes in labor force participation" that have taken place in the United States since 1940. Even within the

9

particular field of demographic concerns, other trends have been noted that would appear to depress the participation rates of women. As Oppenheimer (1970:27) describes the situation for both the 1940-1950 and 1950-1960 periods: "there was more of an increase to explain after the demographic variables had been taken into account." More specifically, she states (1970:27):

> The shifts in population composition cannot account for the increased female work rate primarily because trends in marriage and age structure have operated to put higher proportions of white women into categories which usually have lower rates. The negative effect of these variables has far outweighed the positive effect of continued urbanization.

By way of an alternative, Oppenheimer suggests a purely economic explanation of supply and demand for the increase in total female work rates, and concludes (1970:187) that demand for female labor appears to be "the dominant factor in the situation." Or, as she states (1970:187): "the most likely explanation of the postwar rise in the female work rate is that an increasing number of women have been drawn into the labor force in response to an expansion in job opportunities." However, because the tremendous growth in female labor force participation has been due in large part to the disproportionate increase among women who, traditionally, were not "in demand"--mature married women--a purely economic explanation in terms of demand and supply factors is too simplistic. And, Oppenheimer herself cautions (1970:188) that "because a moderate growth in the female labor force as a whole has depended on a very rapid growth in the work propensities of particular kinds of women, the situation is more complicated than this view suggests."

Many have elaborated this complication of "work propensities" by introducing the element of "choice" or decision-making behavior into the economic analysis of labor force participation. For example, in application of "the general theory of choice" to labor force participation, Bowen and Finegan suggest (1969:16) that decisions concerning labor force entrance are "determined by four broad classes of variables; (1) tastes, (2) expected market earnings rates, (3) expected non-market earnings rates, and (4) the household's total resource constraint." The notion here is that the labor force status of each household member is determined by decisions concerning the allocation of time in the household unit, decisions which take into account the circumstances of other family members. Whether or not a wife enters the labor force would thus be based on considerations of the rewards to be gained from her time invested in market activities weighed against the costs of "substituting" her non-market activities in the home.

McNally (1968:209-210) describes this type of approach to the labor force participation of wives as follows:

> ...married women weigh work for compensation, leisure, and work in the home, and choose among these alternative uses of their time on the basis of rewards and costs of the alternatives to themselves and to their families. These decisions in turn depend on a variety of measurable and unmeasurable considerations.

The measurable considerations frequently identified in such studies include: husband's income, the market wage of the wife, the educational attainment of the wife, the presence of children in the home, unemployment rates, and the availability of jobs for the wife or the "femininity" of job opportunitites. Husband's income is a measure of family resources and indicates the extent to which the wife and other family members can enjoy leisure type activities and obtain valued goods and services without the necessity for additional income.[2] The market wage of the wife is a measure of the "substitution effect." The greater the possible earnings of a wife from employment outside the home, the greater the returns from labor force activity relative to the costs of participation. The educational attainment of the wife is also a measure of the substitution effect: high attainment constitutes a positive effect for working or, alternatively, a negative effect for staying home. As McNally (1968:209) observes:

> [T]he more highly educated women are, the more likely they are to be in the labor force, because they can command more interesting jobs, usually better pay, and make use of their training, avoiding some of the duller activities connected with homemaking.

11

The presence of children in the home is a negative substitution effect, because alternative sources of care for children are often costly and sometimes unavailable. A high unemployment rate suggests negative substitution effect as it pertains to general job prospects for wives. On the other hand, good job prospects for women, as they are reflected in a high proportion of "feminine" job opportunities, constitute a positive substitution effect.[3] In general, the variables directly related to labor force rates for married women are (1) average earnings, (2) education, and (3) the "femininity" of job opportunities. The factors associated with lower rates are (1) high income of husbands, (2) the presence of children, especially small children, in the home, and (3) high unemployment rates (see McNally, 1968:210). The most important positive factor is that of earnings, while the most important negative consideration is that of small children in the home.

More specifically, in regard to the increase in the participation rate of married women over the period 1948 to 1965, Bowen and Finegan (1969:240) conclude that the trend is "explainable in large part in terms of the net outcome of two sets of forces":

Forces acting to push down participation rates:
(1) the increase in the proportion of married women having pre-school children (which has more than offset the effects of rural-urban migration);
(2) a somewhat higher overall unemployment rate at the end of the period than at the beginning;
(3) the increased ability to afford leisure made possible by the increase in the level of real income;
(4) increases in the cost of domestic service;

An even stronger set of forces acting to push up participation rates:
(1) the general increase in female wage rates;
(2) the rise in the educational attainment of women;
(3) the increase in the femininity of the industry mix;

12

(4) the decline in average hours worked per
week and the concomitant increase in the
availability of part-time jobs;
(5) changes in the methods of producing home
goods which have served to encourage the wife
to seek work in the market; and
(6) rising income aspirations.

Bowen and Finegan state (1969:213) that "among all of
the job-incentive variables, the earnings of females
has [sic] had by far the most powerful impact on the
trend in the participation of married women."

McNally (1968:206) also stresses the importance
of income as a determinant for the increased
participation rates of married females while taking
into consideration the "relatively small monetary
returns" gained by women from their economic pursuits
outside the home. The median figure for incomes of
women income recipients rose from $1,017 in 1947 to
$1,638 in 1966--something less than a spectacular
increase. Indeed in 1966, the median income of women
averaged only about 30 percent of that for men,
although in 1947 it was 45 percent of that for men.
So, she asks (1969:206) why women, in particular
married women, have flocked into the labor force for
relatively small monetary gains? Part of the answer
she suggests, but not all, may be in the figures for
family income:

In 1966, families whose heads were married
men averaged $7,838 income. Those in which
the wife was in the paid labor force averaged
$9,246, or about $2,100 more than families
with the wife not in the paid labor force.
The medians do not reflect the extent of the
difference, however. Some 43.3 percent of
families in which the wife worked for pay had
incomes of $10,000 or more, whereas only 26.3
percent with nonworking wives were so
affluent. Wives contribute about one-quarter
of the family income at this level.

Hence, McNally suggests that while the earnings of
working women may not have increased their independence
and power over the years, those earnings may,
nevertheless, have been important contributions to the
total income available for family living.

Although Bowen and Finegan, and others using this
econometric approach have moved toward an analysis of

13

the increased representation of married women in the labor force, they have not been able to explain fully why married women have "flocked into the labor force." Ultimately, Bowen and Finegan (1969:240) acknowledge the influence of unmeasured "changes in attitudes," which they suggest may have had a particularly important impact on the increase in the participation of married women in recent years.[4] In summary, McNally assesses the outcome from this type of research as still far from providing "complete answers to the problem of predicting the size of the female labor force and understanding its fluctuations." And she states (1968:211) that "we must still fall back on the, as yet, nonquantifiable changes and variations in institutional forces and in tastes, aspirations, and other psychological considerations to interpret changes over time."

The measurable economic factors identified above can, however, explain more of the variation in the labor force status of married women at a single point in time. It is to a consideration of these cross-sectional studies that we now turn.

Who Enters?

Womanpower is one of our country's greatest resources. Women's skills and abilities are being used more fully and more creatively than ever before--in the home, in the community, and on the job (Womens Bureau, 1969:5).

Which women bring their skills and abilities to a job outside the home? Or, stated another way, which women enter the labor force? Oppenheimer (1970:19) suggests that "at least with regard to age, marital, and family status, the female labor force today is not very different from the adult female population as a whole." Others (notably Cain, 1966; Mahoney, 1961; Mincer, 1962; Sweet, 1973) focusing on the determinants of labor force status for married women at a given point in time have concluded that family status and life cycle variables are important influences.

In 1961, Weil (1961:93-94) found attitudinal variables, in particular, attitudes of husbands toward wives' outside employment, to be more closely related to the actual and planned participation of wives than several economic considerations. Contrary to

14

expectations, she found that differential availability of employment, high socioeconomic status of the family, wife's work status before marriage, family debts, and the planned purchase of major items, showed little or no relationship to either actual or planned labor force activity. Placing her findings in a context of marital roles for wives, Weil (1961:93) concluded that "a woman will perform or plan to perform in both the traditional and career roles or the companionship and career roles:

1. When her husband's attitude toward her outside employment is positive. (r_{tet} = .92 for actual participation)

2. When she performed in an occupation before marriage which required high educational achievement or specialized training. (r_{tet} = .72 for actual participation)

3. When the woman continued to work after marriage. (r_{tet} = .60 for actual participation)

4. When the woman has achieved a high professional level or has specialized training. (r_{tet} = .56 and .43 for actual participation)

5. When her husband accepts an obligation for child care and household chores. (r_{tet} = .55 and .41 for actual participation)

6. When her children are of school age. (r_{tet} = .27 for actual participation)

Morgan, et al., (1962) also found husbands' attitudes to be the best predictor of the employment of wives.

Unfortunately, most systematic studies of women's entrance into the labor force have not had access to such attitudinal data. They have, nonetheless, been able to explain the variation in married women's labor force status, particularly among areas at a given point in time, by using eco-demographic variables. At the individual level, Cain reports (1966:114-115) that "most of the variation in labor force behavior could be explained on the basis of the presence and number of children and the age of the wife." As for the "explanatory power" of the age variable, it is common knowledge today that there are "peaks" in the labor force participation of married women, "with an early peak before families are begun and a later peak in middle age" (McNally, 1968:210). More specifically, Bowen and Finegan (1969:541-542) relate:

> There is a double peak in the female curve, the first occurring around the ages of 18-19 and 20-24, and the second occurring at the 45-54 age level. At each of these two peaks, roughly half of all women are in the labor force. The most pronounced part of the intervening dip comes at the 25-34 age level, when homemaking, childbearing, and the raising of young children tend to discourage the labor force participation of American women.

In an early study of white husband-wife families in St. Paul, Minnesota, Mahoney (1961) was able to explain 56 percent of the variation in labor force status among wives using 15 variables, which he divided into three categories of (a) economic variables, (b) family characteristics, and (c) personal characteristics of the wife. He found (1961:576) that "the variable most predictive of labor force participation among married women over age 29 is past employment experience." When the effects of that variable were removed, the presence of small children became the single most predictive variable. However, his findings varied by the age of women, and Mahoney stressed the importance of the "concept of family cycle." He concluded (1961:576):

> If we can generalize from these cross-sectional data, it would appear that young married women seek employment for a variety of reasons including family economic pressure. The birth of children places a premium upon the wife's presence in the home, and the mother who continues to work does so because of strong feelings that such employment contributes to personal and family welfare.

Hence, Mahoney (a) suggested the possible importance of economic factors underlying the work decisions of married women, which pertain to the "economic necessity" for working and (b) recognized that these factors may vary according to the stage of the family lifecycle.[5]

Differential employment rates for wives by the income of their husbands' have frequently been observed (see Sweet, 1973:6). In general, those observations seem to support the importance of economic necessity as a "precipitating conditions" (Sobol, 1963) for the entrance of married women into the labor force, particularly married women aged 35 to 44 who are in the high "familial demand" category. In 1960, around 40 percent of women 35 to 44 who were married to men with income of less than $4,000 were at work, contrasted to only 17 percent of women who were married to men with incomes of $10,000 or more (Sweet, 1973:6). In the 1955 Growth of American Families study (on results from the GAF survey see Cain, 1966; Sobol, 1963; Sweet, 1973), nearly four-fifths of the working wives reported that they were working for predominantly economic reasons. Of wives whose husbands' incomes were less than $3,000, 58 percent reported that they were working because of "chronic or temporary financial problems." That percentage decreased to 17 for those wives whose husbands' incomes were $7,000 or more. Consistent with the suggestion of Mahoney (1961:576), economic reasons were more important for working mothers with young children in the home.

Also supporting the notion of Mahoney (1961) regarding the increased importance of economic necessity for work decisions at certain stages of the family life-cycle are results from another survey. In a 1964 study undertaken by the U.S. Bureau of the Census on women who had either taken jobs or stopped working in 1963 (see Rosenfeld and Parrella, 1965:1077-1078), 44.9 percent of the 225,000 women between the ages of 35 and 44 reported "financial necessity" as the most important reason they entered the labor force. The figure was approximately the same for women 25 to 34 (45.0), but substantially higher than the figures for women 18 to 24 (38.2) and for women 45 to 64 (34.0). The women giving "financial necessity" as the primary motive for entering the labor force were disproportionately represented in the following categories: those with children under 6 years of age, those with less than 12 years of school, and those whose husbands earned less than $60 a week. On the other hand, the women who gave "personal satisfaction" as their primary reason for working tended to be those with no children under 6, those with 1 year of college or more, and those married to high earners of $100 or more a week.

In summarizing the documented differentials in

17

the employment rates of American wives, Sweet
(1973:136) states that the probability of employment is
greater (a) the greater the level of family economic
need and (b) the greater the employability and earning
capacity of wives as indexed by educational
attainments. The probability of employment is lower
when women's familial responsibilities are greater, as
indexed by the age and number of children in the
family. However, he notes that the probabilities are
conditioned by the age or life-cycle stage of women and
also by the ethnic status of women. He points out
(1973:51-52) several ways in which age is relevant to
the labor force activity of women:

1. Age is correlated with physical capacity
to work. The older a woman, the higher the
probability that she is physically unable to
work.
2. Age has a life cycle aspect having to do
with the need for income. A young woman who
is married but has no children is likely to
wish to work in order to accumulate assets in
the form of a house or durable goods. An
older woman can, to a certain extent, merely
live on accumulated assets and durables
without the need to work. Women between 40
and 60 who have children in the household may
well be supporting a child who is living
outside the household (e.g., a child in
college).
3. Age locates a woman in a cohort, the
members of which have lived through
comparable periods of their lives in the same
historical environment. There has been a
trend in the employment of women in the
United States such that the younger a woman
is, the more likely she is to have been
exposed to employment at any given earlier
stage of her life. In addition, World War II
was a historical event that had a marked
accelerating effect on the previously slow
trend in the increase in labor force
participation. Women who completed their
education immediately before the rapid
increase in employment opportunities should
probably show the influence of this event on
their current labor force activity, at least
if the idea of persistence has any validity.
4. In considering the question of whether or
not a woman ever worked, age is relevant (in
determining the period of exposure) to the

18

possibility of ever having worked.

The points regarding age are elaborated here to give an indication of the more subtle as well as the obvious impact of age on possible labor force participation.

In addition to the contingency of age, Sweet (1973:52) also addresses the mitigating influence of ethnicity: "Nonwhite wives have repeatedly been observed to have higher rates of employment than white wives. These differences appear to persist when other relevant characteristics are controlled." One of the reasons Cain (1966:119-120) offers for the higher participation level of nonwhite wives (even when small children are present) is that of "the relative instability of nonwhite families" which leads the nonwhite wife "to maintain closer ties to the labor market." In this regard, higher rates of employment have been observed for both black and white women married more than once (see for example, Sweet, 1973:24, 105-107). Sweet (1973) suggests that the difference in the salience and content of husbands' attitudes toward the employment of wives may also be contributing factors to the greater employment of black mothers. He states (1973:101): "Black husbands may, on average, be less likely to have such negative attitudes (see Morgan, et al., 1966:326-333) and, to the extent that they do have them, be less influential."

When the positive and negative effects of the measurable eco-demographic variables pertaining to substitution ("enabling and facilitating conditions") and economic necessity ("precipating conditions") are considered, it has not been unusual for recent efforts in the field to account for 60 to 70 percent of cross-sectional variation in the participation rates of married women, specifically, variation among metropolitan areas (see for example Bowen and Finegan, 1969:191, 772-860). This leaves approximately one-third of the variation to be explained even in the more successful efforts, and the unexplained "residual" is very often attributed to missing information on attitudinal variations among women and to differences in other unmeasured variables such as tastes. Efforts to explain disaggregated data have been somewhat less conclusive when the effects of age variation are removed and, again, the less than perfect explanatory power has heralded calls for data on previously unmeasured (and presently unmeasurable) phenomena such as tastes.

However, in his cumulative investigation into the labor force participation of married women, Sweet suggests a deficit in our knowledge about the determinants of participation that may be more readily overcome with existing data--namely, knowledge on how differences in employment patterns among women account for such a phenomenon as variation in the earnings effect. He states (1973:163):

> What proportion of the population are in careers; what proportion of women are sporadic entrants into the labor force; what proportion of women remain in the labor force over long periods but never experience any occupation advancement or income increase, apart from compensation for inflation? More important than what proportion of women are found in each of these circumstances are the characteristics which differentiate women with sporadic labor force involvement from those with long-term involvement or differentiate those in careers from those in dead-end positions.

This cursory review of existing knowledge about women's labor force participation has been offered to highlight the present need to deal with questions concerning women's careers. Since the work of Bancroft in 1958 and of Mincer in 1962, we have refined but not substantially increased our ability to explain the participation of women in labors for pay or profit either through time or at a given point in time. At least part of the problem that Sweet identifies may lie in the current tendency to treat women "entrants" as an undifferentiated category of participants.

Summary and Continuations

Women comprise a larger segment of American "manpower" than ever before as proportionately more and more females are entering the labor force. By 1980, three out of five women were employed in the labor force and two out of five workers were women. Moreover, nine out of ten adult females had been, were then, or would be engaged in extra-familial sustenance activities. In other words, most women have participated or will participate in the American occupational structure. Accordingly, any complete description of that structure must include an analysis of female occupational patterns.

Because of the increased importance of woman-power, a growing body of scholars has recently turned attention to finding the determinants for female labor force activity, especially for the activity of married women. The conclusion has been that some married women are more likely to be found in the labor force than others at a given point in time. On the one hand, women with high earnings potential are more likely to enter than those with low earnings and educational attainments, ceteris paribus. On the other hand, married women are more likely to work for reasons of economic necessity, within certain age ranges. The presence of small children is a decisive deterrent to participation, although more decisive at certain ages and more a deterrent for white women than for black women.

As a possible explanation for the deficiencies in previous explanation, it is suggested that the problem may lie in the effort to find one set of determinants for female labor force status--a problematic dependent variable. The orientation prompting the efforts to determine labor force status on the basis of a single set of regression equations seems somewhat along the lines of "ah ha, these are all women and therefore certainly alike in their participation patterns." Of course, we "know" that women are all alike! The assumptions guiding this investigation are somewhat different. There may indeed be orderly patterns in the variegations of human beings (in this case, in the ways that women participate in the labor force), but that is an empirical question. Such order should be sought empirically rather than assumed.

To know that x number of women are in the labor force at a given point in time is to know very little about the nature of their participation--about how they participate--and differences in the nature of participation suggest that the determinants of participation differ. For example, consider five females who are designated as in the labor force at a given point in time but who have very different participation patterns. One participates full-time and year around as an architect and has been in the labor force since leaving school. Another participates as a nurse four evenings a week and plans to quit her job when her first child is born. The third participates as an elementary school teacher and has just re-entered the labor force after seventeen years as a homemaker because her youngest child is now in high school and money is needed for college educations. The fourth is

21

employed as a part-time mail clerk while taking college courses toward a degree in home economics and until the "right man comes along." The fifth is seeking employment for the first time after 20 years of homemaking because the "right man" turned out to be more right for another woman, and his support does not meet present needs.

To say that these women are all in the labor force at a given point in time is not to say that they all participate in the same manner. On the contrary, the character of female participation in the labor force is highly variable, and that variablity must somehow be taken into account in the search for determining factors.

Notes
Chapter One

[1]For a review and assessment of the divergence in findings, see Oppenheimer (1970:2-6).

[2]Although "leisure type activities" for the wife are often assumed, an alternative interpretation is that the wife is engaged in supportive familial activities, in particular, activities in support of the husband's occupation or career. Such activities might include community service, job-related social functions, religious and political activities, which could be essential in furthering the husband's career.

[3]Ethnic status and age are often used as control variables. In addition, age is used to gauge the life-cycle stage of the family and so to measure potential productivity as well as the needs of a family unit. On the importance of age as a "moderator variable" see Mahoney (1961:576-577) and the comments of Sweet presented on pages 18-19 of this chapter.

[4]Furthermore, as with many of the major studies of economic influences on the secular changes in the labor force participation rates of married women, the results of Bowen and Finegan are based on the analysis of cross-sectional rather than time series data. In other words, they use "cross-sectional regression coefficients" (Bowen and Finegan, 1969:241) to explain changes through time. There remains considerable controversy in the literature as to the applicability of regression coefficients obtained from cross-sectional findings in explaining changes through time

(see Cain, 1966:118; McNally, 1968:210-211; Mincer, 1966:91).

[5]Regarding the importance of family life-cycle stages, Sweet (1973:132) states "The importance of including family status, or stage in the family life cycle, as a variable in any model of the employment of wives is clear. Not only does this family variable exert an influence on employment, independent of the "economic" variables, education and income adequacy, but more importantly the stage in the family life cycle conditions and constrains the effects of the economic variables on employment."

CHAPTER TWO

DIFFERENCES BETWEEN THE MARKETPLACE
PATTERNS OF WOMEN AND MEN

Some women participate in the labor force as a career, meaning in a manner similar to men. They participate continuously and full time and have the same expectations and aspirations regarding extra-familial occupational activities as do males. On the other hand, many women do not participate in the labor force as a career. They participate only irregularly, entering and leaving the labor force in response to familial circumstances and demands, and when they do participate they enter occupations that are considered "uniquely compatible with the female nature" (on this subject see Dahlstrom, 1971; Epstein, 1970; Knudsen, 1969; Smuts, 1971 ed.). For many women, participation in the American occupational structure is conditioned by and contingent on expectations associated with the traditional wife-mother-homemaker role, and these expectations conflict with the expectations associated with an extra-familial career.

Evidence of previous studies regarding differences between the participation patterns of women and men provides a preview of important differences that are relevant in contemplating differences in occupational patterns among women. However, results from those investigations have seldom informed recent efforts to find determinants for female labor force status nor informed initial attempts to explore female occupational mobility (on this issue see Havens and Tully, 1972; Rogoff-Ramsøy, 1974). There appears to have been an unfortunate "twain" between the two streams of inquiry--unfortunate because documentable differences in the participation patterns of females are crucial in seeking determinants for female labor force participation and for assessing patterns of occupational movement among females.

Most previous investigations into patterns of female labor force participation have focused on the differences between females and males and on causes and consequences of those observed differences. The primary differences can be categorized as differences in (1) the extent or continuity of work experience and (2) the status of occupations or the rewards derived from participation. The first difference involves the disproportionate number of women who participate as "secondary workers." The difference in rewards is thought to result from this tendency for secondary participation (see Polachek, 1975) as well as from the disproportionate representation of women in low paid "sex-typed" female occupations.

The Regularity of Labor Force Participation

Some men in their active years enter and leave the labor force from time to time, or work part time rather than full time. The vast majority of adult men, however, remain more or less steadily in the labor force until they retire. Moreover, a man is likely to be not only a member of the labor force, but actually holding a full-time job unless he is ill, is on vacation, out on strike, or has left or lost his job and not yet found another. Although a few women work steadily from the time they leave school until they retire, the pattern for most women is markedly different (National Manpower Council, 1957:49).

The oft-noted participation pattern for women is that they tend to enter the labor force after completing school, leave upon getting married or when the first child is born, and return in later years or "leave and re-enter employment several times in later years in response to the needs of their families" (National Manpower Council, 1957:49). To explain this difference in the patterns of employment between men and women, many have suggested that "most women are not the principal breadwinners of their families" (National Manpower Council, 1957:49). As Bancroft (1958:118) describes the situation: for men, secondary workers are a small minority of the employed, whereas for women, the great majority of the employed are secondary workers. "Secondary workers" are defined (Bancroft, 1958:118) as "workers other than family heads or principal earners." Family heads tend to be "year-round, full-time workers," but other family members tend to "work only part of the year, or on a part-time basis, if they work at all" (Bancroft, 1958:113).

26

In 1958, Bancroft reported (1958:113) that only "13.1 percent of the wives of family heads" worked full time every week. In 1968, Ginzberg concluded (1968:194) that "most women who hold jobs work less than full time." He reported (1968:194): "Of the 33.8 million women who worked in 1965, 13.1 million, or about 39 percent worked full time, full year. About 10 million worked full time for less than a full year, and another 10.6 million worked part time throughout or for part of the year." Data for 1967 similarly revealed that women were much more likely than men to work part time or part of the year (Women's Bureau, 1969:55). However, in some part because of changing definitions, the majority of employed women now work full-time.

Very little has been accomplished regarding the determinants of female participation apart from labor force status at a given point in time. However, there is some recent evidence which indicates that women with high educational attainments are not only more likely to enter the labor force, they are also more likely to work 35 hours a week or more, i.e., full-time (see Sweet, 1973:38-41). In addition, Sweet reports (1973:136):

> Some analysis of the determinants of hours worked has also been reported. In general, the same factors that increase the probability of employment (high family economic pressure, high education, and minimal familial responsibilities), also increase the conditional probability of working full time (Morgan, et al., 1962, Chap. 11).

Preliminary findings from NLS data on women 30 to 44, which elaborate some of the conditions for the probabilities referred to by Sweet, can be summarized as follows (U.S. Department of Labor, 1970:129-135):

> Irrespective of the presence of children, employed married women are more likely to work part time than those who are not married. . . . The only exception to this generalization occurs among nonmarried black women with children under six years of age, who are actually somewhat more likely to be working part time than their married counterparts.

> The presence of children apparently

27

exerts an independent influence on number of hours worked only in the case of married white women and nonmarried black. Among married white women who are employed, those with children under 18 in the home are twice as likely as others to be part-time workers. Among nonmarried blacks, those with children under six are twice as likely as those with no children to be part-time workers, although there is not much difference between the latter and those whose youngest child is over six.

To some extent whether a married white woman works full time or part time appears to depend on the relative need of her family for income. Those who work part time are from families in which the median income (without the respondent's earnings) is $8,226 compared to $7,400 for those who work full time. . . . Among black women, however, the relationship is reversed; there is somewhat greater tendency for full-time workers to come from families with higher annual incomes (exclusive of the respondent's earnings).

Using two measures of labor force attachment--employment experience in 1966 and percentage of years since leaving school in which respondents worked at least six months--it is evident that part-time workers have displayed a weaker attachment to the labor force in the past than have full-time workers.
. . . there is no consistent relationship between hourly rate of pay and hours usually worked within the major occupation groups containing sufficient sample cases to permit generalization.
. . . part-time workers are less likely than full-time workers to require child-care arrangements if at all. . . . Moreover, of those who do require such arrangements, part-time workers are much more likely to be able to arrange for the care of their children without cost.

Finally, there is also evidence to support the hypothesis that part-time workers spend less time and money getting to work than do full-time workers.

The number of weeks worked by respondents in 1966 was related to: good health of respondents, bad health of respondents, bad health of husbands for married white respondents (although not for married black respondents), vocational courses in high school for black respondents (although not for white), professional or trade certification, "permissive" attitudes toward the employment of mother, disliking for child-care and housework, and favorable attitudes of husbands.

Of course, unmarried women are prone to participate more regularly than secondary workers (see Ginzberg, 1968:194; Sawhill, 1973:388; Women's Bureau, 1969:66) with the exception of never-married women in the younger age brackets, but in 1968 almost 3 out of 5 women workers were married with husbands present, and Sweet (1973:29) suggests "that the career wife is very rare in the population."[1] So although unmarried women comprise a considerable part of female representation in the labor force, especially in the professional categories, the modal patterns of female participation reflect the greater number of married women--women who frequently are irregular participants in the American occupational structure.

The Rewards Derived from Participation

Women gain less from participation than do men. Such differences persist between women and men who work full time the year around, who have the same educational attainments, who are the same age, and who are employed in the same occupational categories and even the same jobs. Moreover the gap in earnings is widening (Women's Bureau, 1969:133-134). Table 2.1 reports sex differentials between full-time year-around workers for each year between 1955 and 1970. The widening of the earnings gap between 1955 and 1970 cannot, therefore, be attributed to differences in hours and weeks worked between females and males.

Regarding another possible explanation for the difference in occupational rewards for women and men, that of educational differences, Fuchs (1971:9) has observed that "for equal years of schooling, the male-female differential in hourly earnings is much larger than the differential between whites and blacks." Table 2.2 relates the female-male differences in median income by educational level. Again, the comparisons are for full-time year-around workers and hence the

TABLE 2.1: MEDIAN EARNINGS OF FULL-TIME, YEAR ROUND WORKERS, BY SEX, 1955-1977 (PERSONS 14 YEARS OF AGE AND OVER)

Year	Median Earnings		Women's median earnings as percent of men's
	Women	Men	
1977	8,618	14,626	58.9
1976	8,099	13,455	60.2
1975	7,504	12,758	58.8
1974	6,772	11,835	57.2
1973	6,335	11,186	56.6
1972	5,903	10,202	57.9
1971	5,593	9,399	59.5
1970	5,323	8,966	59.4
1969	4,977	8,227	60.5
1968	4,457	7,664	58.2
1967	4,150	7,182	57.8
1966	3,973	6,848	58.0
1965	3,823	6,375	60.0
1964	3,690	6,195	59.6
1963	3,561	5,978	59.6
1962	3,446	5,974	59.5
1961	3,351	5,644	59.4
1960	3,293	5,417	60.8
1959	3,193	5,209	61.3
1958	3,102	4,927	63.0
1957	3,008	4,713	63.8
1956	2,827	4,466	63.3
1955	2,719	4,252	63.9

Source: U.S. Department of Labor, Women's Bureau (1979:6)

differences cannot be dismissed on the grounds that those women are part-time and/or temporary workers. An interesting observation is that women are better off (relative to men) in the highest and lowest levels of educational attainment. Such is, perhaps, indicative of greater income parity between women and men in the highest and lowest occupational categories.

The idea of greater income parity at the higher occupational levels is borne out by the statistics presented in Table 2.3. However, the findings for gross occupational categories do not support the notion of greater income parity at the lower occupational levels. Furthermore, the gap between women and men is not less than 30 percent for any category. Why?

Ginzberg (1968:195-196) observes that there is an earnings discrepancy by sex in each major occupational category with women employed in the less remunerative branches. And Cohen (1971:434) concludes that, "The most important reason for the difference in the average pay of men and women is the clustering of women in lower paying jobs." These are "sex-typed" female jobs, meaning that they are held predominantly by women, and according to many reports (see for example, Oppenheimer, 1968; Weisskoff, 1972), the tendency of women workers to cluster in such jobs has not changed markedly since the turn of the century. Table 2.4 documents this tendency of women to cluster in certain jobs within broad occupational categories, more specifically, in the less rewarding jobs. Females are disproportionately overrepresented in the lower status and lower paid occupations within major categories (see Havens and Tully, 1972:774-775). For example, using a ratio of percent female in the professional category to the percentage of males in that category, females are underrepresented in the following jobs (among the highest paying in the professional category): physicians and surgeons, dentists, lawyers and judges, and architects. However, females are overrepresented in these professional jobs (among the lowest paying in the professional category): social workers, elementary teachers, librarians, nurses, and medical and dental technicians. Similar patterns exist within the clerical, sales, operative, and service categories.

The question remains why women are concentrated in lower paid jobs within broad occupational categories. One explanation is that of supply and demand (Weisskoff, 1972:165):

TABLE 2.2: MEDIAN INCOME IN 1970 OF FULL-TIME YEAR-ROUND WORKERS, BY SEX AND YEARS OF SCHOOL COMPLETED (PERSONS 25 YEARS OF AGE AND OVER)

Years of school completed	Median income		Women's median earnings as percent of men's
	Women	Men	
College			
5 years or more	$9,581	$14,747	65.0
4 years	8,156	13,264	61.5
1-3 years	6,604	11,183	59.1
High School			
4 years	5,580	9,567	58.3
1-3 years	4,644	8,514	54.7
Elementary School			
8 years	4,181	7,535	55.5
7 years or less	3,798	6,043	62.8

Derived from Women's Bureau (1971:3). Source: U.S. Department of Commerce, Bureau of the Census: Current Population Reports, P-60, No. 80.

TABLE 2.3: MEDIAN EARNINGS IN 1970 OF YEAR-ROUND WORKERS, BY SEX AND MAJOR OCCUPATIONAL GROUPING (PERSONS 25 YEARS TO 64 YEARS)

	Median Earnings		Women's median earnings as percent of men's
	Women[1]	Men[2]	
Professional, technical and kindred workers	$7,172	$12,237	58.6
Managers and administrators except farm	6,246	12,101	51.6
Craftsmen and kindred workers	5,370	9,034	59.4
Clerical and kindred workers	5,366	8,536	62.9
Transport equipment operatives	4,898	7,955	61.6
Operatives except transport	4,432	7,863	56.4
Laborers except farm	4,170	6,646	62.7
Sales workers	3,809	10,093	37.7
Service workers except private household	3,666	6,857	53.5
Farmers and farm managers	2,876	5,561	51.7
Farm laborers and farm foremen	2,595	4,147	62.6
Private household workers	1,792	3,549	50.5

[1] Source: U.S. Bureau of Census (1973:Table 7)
[2] Source: U.S. Bureau of Census (1973:Table 1).

33

TABLE 2.4: OCCUPATION BY PARTICIPATION, EARNINGS, AND SEX, 1960

Occupation	Total with earnings¹		Worked 50-52 weeks¹		% by column 50-52 weeks		Ratio F%/M%	Median earnings worked 50-52 weeks²			
	Female	Male	Female	Male	Female	Male		Female	(n)	Male	(n)
PROFESSIONAL	2,604,128	4,465,102	987,512	3,462,300	.102	.119	.857	4,186	(1)	7,124	(1)
Physicians & Surgeons	14,736	212,163	8,791	165,535	.0009	.0037	.159	6,562	(1.1)	14,704	(1.1)
Dentists	1,718	84,383	760	50,588	.0000	.0017	.000	...		12,219	(1.2)
Lawyers & Judges	6,992	199,407	4,807	172,468	.0005	.0059	.085	5,681	(1.4)	10,981	(1.3)
Architects	658	29,248	359	25,392	.0000	.0009	.000	...		9,094	(1.4)
Engineers	7,572	856,803	5,832	765,436	.0006	.0262	.023	6,049	(1.2)	8,515	(1.5)
College P.,P.,I.	34,850	134,813	11,456	78,467	.0012	.0027	.447	5,814	(1.3)	7,971	(1.6)
Natural Scientists	14,074	134,233	9,734	117,580	.0010	.0040	.248	5,535	(1.5)	7,700	(1.7)
Teachers, Sec.	232,263	269,555	43,523	126,120	.0045	.0043	1.042	4,931	(1.6)	6,328	(1.8)
Technicians: El. & El.	4,479	88,713	3,376	73,289	.0004	.0025	.159	4,248	(1.9)	6,214	(1.9)
Technicians: Eng. & P.	23,276	164,252	16,084	132,542	.0017	.0045	.375	4,179	(1.10)	5,953	(1.10)
Teachers, NEC	85,151	56,467	22,743	32,980	.0024	.0011	2.126	3,834	(1.12)	5,952	(1.11)
Teachers, El.	823,476	139,689	136,598	59,606	.0142	.0020	6.958	4,559	(1.8)	5,635	(1.12)
Social Workers	59,048	34,478	42,623	27,500	.0044	.0009	4.671	4,654	(1.7)	5,607	(1.13)
Musicians & Teachers	104,295	83,503	28,040	35,577	.0029	.0012	2.381	1,503	(1.15)	5,478	(1.14)
Librarians	69,860	11,990	39,139	7,180	.0041	.0002	16.679	4,164	(1.11)	5,403	(1.15)
Technicians: M & D	83,404	52,188	53,904	41,134	.0056	.0014	3.976	3,670	(1.14)	4,892	(1.16)
Nurses, Prof.	545,781	14,006	292,984	10,460	.0304	.0004	84.889	3,930	(1.13)	4,586	(1.17)
Nurses, St. Prof.	29,937	772	5,934	320	.0006	.0000	—	893	(1.16)	...	
MANAGERS	683,750	4,604,044	514,601	4,024,244	.053	.138	.384	3,800	(2)	6,926	(2)
NEC-Salaried	335,801	2,239,549	239,606	2,006,612	.0248	.0687	.360	4,221	(2.1)	7,544	(2.1)
NEC-Self Employed	208,086	1,641,648	156,984	1,380,016	.0163	.0472	.345	2,722	(2.2)	6,010	(2.2)
CRAFTSMEN	249,547	8,053,112	149,616	6,020,344	.016	.206	.077	3,555	(3)	5,699	(3)
CLERICAL	6,042,172	3,074,643	3,885,181	2,347,915	.403	.080	5.038	3,546	(4)	5,205	(5)
Agents NEC	36,500	131,213	16,934	112,454	.0017	.0038	.442	4,156	(4.2)	6,366	(5.1)
Ins. Adjusters	6,686	49,060	5,142	42,496	.0005	.0014	.344	3,849	(4.5)	5,844	(5.2)
Telephone Ops.	338,288	15,940	225,134	10,901	.0233	.0004	61.431	3,599	(4.10)	5,790	(5.3)
Ticket Agents	15,732	56,243	10,894	48,243	.0011	.0016	.646	4,405	(4.11)	5,736	(5.4)
Secretaries	1,385,864	40,953	955,844	34,028	.0991	.0012	85.065	3,812	(4.6)	5,733	(5.5)
Clerical NEC-Mgf.	384,957	415,550	253,485	323,443	.0263	.0111	2.335	3,677	(4.8)	5,637	(5.6)
Dispatchers	5,785	51,610	3,541	42,180	.0004	.0014	.276	3,039	(4.19)	5,606	(5.7)
Stenographers	254,237	11,810	171,351	9,450	.0178	.0003	55.017	3,742	(4.7)	5,578	(5.8)
Postal Clerks	34,565	179,804	22,946	153,398	.0024	.0052	.476	4,099	(4.3)	5,571	(5.9)
Mail Carriers	3,835	196,052	1,917	168,903	.0002	.0058	.035	3,569	(4.11)	5,379	(5.10)
Payroll Clerks	64,025	43,981	49,141	34,059	.0051	.0012	4.374	3,909	(4.4)	5,361	(5.11)
Office Machine Ops.	224,792	80,679	146,087	63,157	.0152	.0022	7.030	3,674	(4.9)	5,134	(5.12)
Bookkeepers	710,795	153,396	494,039	121,314	.0512	.0042	12.317	3,414	(4.13)	4,836	(5.13)

34

TABLE 2.5: FEMALE AVERAGE HOURLY EARNINGS RELATIVE TO MALE FOR ALL NONFARM EMPLOYED AND SELECTED SUBGROUPS, BY AGE, 1959

Age Characteristic	Unadjusted Ratio	Ratio[1]	Ratio[2]
Less than 25	83	82	82
25 to 34	69	69	73
35 to 44	58	59	62
45 to 54	58	57	61
55 to 64	57	54	61

Derived from Fuchs (1971:10, Table 1).

[1] Adjusted for color, city size and schooling.

[2] Adjusted for color, schooling, city size, marital status, class of worker, and length of trip to work.

39

years, whereas the worklife expectancy of a
male of the same age is about 38 years. . . .
Similarly, several studies of the job tenure
of workers have indicated that after age 25
or 30, married women have spent less time on
their current jobs than have men. . . .

She observes (1973:388), that these same statistics
indicate "that single women spend as many or more years
in the labor force and on the job than men do." Yet,
as noted previously (Fuchs, 1971), a gap of about 20
percent still remains between the earnings of men and
single women, as a minimum estimate.

Taking the factor of career continuity into
account, Sawhill (1973:391) concludes that "there
remains a 43 percent differential between men and women
who are similar with respect to age, education, race,
region, hours and weeks worked, and time spent in the
labor force." Similarly, Suter and Miller (1973) find
that if women who were 30 to 44 in 1966, had the same
education and year-around full-time employment in 1966
as men, had the same occupational status as men, and
had worked all their lives, their income would be
increased only to 62 percent of that received by men.
They conclude (1973:211):

While the relationship of income with
socioeconomic characteristics is more
consistent for women than for men, women
receive decidedly lower increments for equal
step increases in educational level and
occupational status. Married women earn
about the same amount as single women with
similar education and work experience. After
all factors are considered, the overall
difference between the earnings of men and
women was about $2,800 in annual wages in
1966 or about 38% of the wages for men.

What reasons can be found for the remaining
difference? To explain his findings of pay differences
between men and women in the same job, Buckley
(1971:38) remarks a problem in job descriptions which
do not take into account "differences in duties that
occur among establishments." For example, an
establishment may "pay men performing heavy janitorial
work more than women with light cleaning duties, but
both would be classified as janitors in the wage
survey." Suffice it to say, this observer believes the
problem of "unequal work" by males and females to be of

doubtful validity, especially in regard to jobs which do not depend on muscles below the neck for their accomplishment. To the contrary, there may well be a problem inherent in job classifications, but at the present time it is more likely to be one of different classifications for men and women who perform similar jobs. Citing "no evidence that employer discrimination is a major direct influence on men-women differentials," Buckley (1971:39) posits a difference in sexual "roles" (as suggested by Fuchs, 1971:14) to explain the earnings gap: "Role differentiation, which begins in the cradle, affects the choice of occupation, labor force attachment, location of work, postschool investment, hours of work, and other variables that influence earnings."

Socialization patterns may, in the last analysis, contain an answer for the fact that men earn more than women--"one of the best established and least satisfactorily explained aspects of American labor market behavior" (Fuchs, 1971:9). Additionally, perceptions of the earnings gap may condition expectations of both employers and employees regarding the participation of women in the American labor force. As an intimation of complex causal interaction, Sweet comments (1973:152):

> The higher wage of full-year workers may reflect their productivity due to their greater commitment to the work role and greater job tenure and work experience, or it may reflect the low rate at which marginal workers can be induced into the work force. On the other hand, labor force turnover and marginality may be due, in part, to the lower rate at which women workers are paid and their marginal position in the work force.

Summary and Continuations

One of the major differences between the labor force participation patterns of females and males is that males are more prone to participate as a career, meaning that more males than females participate in the labor force full time, year around, and continuously throughout their productive lives. Indeed, this difference in the regularity with which males and females tend to participate in the American labor force is often cited to explain another major difference between the occupational patterns of female and males--

41

that of occupational status or the rewards derived from participation. Females are said to achieve less than males and to receive less than males because they do not participate like males.

A major long-term goal of this study is to explain variation in achieved occupational status among women who do participate in a manner similar to that of men. A preliminary set of questions of critical importance thus concerns the ways in which females participate in the American occupational structure. Of the women who do participate, which participate in a manner similar to men--i.e., as a career--and what are the determinants of such participation?

Notes
Chapter Two

[1]Using marital status as a "determinant" for female labor force participation is conventional but quite problematical. Such requires an assumption that marital conditions influence labor force decisions, for example that an unmarried woman enters the labor force because she is unmarried (i.e., because she cannot "catch" or "hold" a man to support her). Obviously, there is another causal sequence which may be relevant--that labor force conditions influence marital decisions. For example, a career woman may choose to be unmarried because she prefers the rewards of work outside the home to the rewards of the wife-mother-homemaker role. Alternatively, a woman may decide to marry and accept the traditional wife-mother-homemaker role because she finds working outside the home relatively unrewarding. There is little doubt that for many women a conflict between the career role and the wife-mother-homemaker role exists, if only because a majority of husbands define the two as incompatible (see Oppenheimer, 1970:40-50). Hence, for many women the pursuit of one means giving up the other (see Safilios-Rothschild, 1974:109). And, it is conceivable that some women, indeed more than a few women, choose to forego or give up the wife-mother-homemaker role in order to pursue careers in the American occupational structure (see Havens, 1971, 1974).

P A R T   II

WOMEN'S CAREER PATTERNS:

An Empirical Analysis

While there have been systematic studies of women's entrance into the labor force and while attention has often focused on the differences between the participation patterns of males and females, very little has been done regarding differences in the nature of labor force participation among women. In other words, few previous studies have explored variability in the character of participation among females who do enter the labor force. Yet answers to questions regarding variability in the nature of participation or involvement among females are prerequisite for attempts to address issues concerning the rewards females gain from their participation in the American occupational structure, in particular, their occupational status. Part Two considers one such variable characteristic of female labor force participation--namely, the "regularity" with which women participate in the labor force. This crucial aspect of women's participation has never been treated systematically as a dependent variable, although some have used certain dimensions of the variable in efforts to explain observed differences between the earnings of women and men in the labor force. Three dimensions of regular participation are identified and discussed in Chapter Three. These dimensions are then compiled into a composite measure of labor force attachment, which is further used to differentiate variable patterns of labor force involvement. Applying this measure to data from the National Longitudinal Surveys of Work Experience, the research continues in Chapter Four with a description of the labor force participation patterns of mature American women and with the exploration of influences on the observed work patterns. In Chapter Five a simple model is presented for assessing the relative impact of the more influential independent variables on the participation patterns of women in the American occupational structure.

CHAPTER THREE

DESCRIBING THE MARKET WORK PATTERNS
OF MATURE WOMEN

As reviewed in Chapter One, previous attempts to explain female labor force participation have focused upon the labor force status of women, i.e., whether or not women are counted as in the labor force at a given point in time. These attempts have ignored much documented variability in the character of female labor force participation. Such conceptual/methodological limitation may account for the limited explanatory success of those previous efforts (usually less than 25 percent of the variation is explained in studies based on observations for individual women).[1] Many women work part-time; many others work 40 or more hours a week. Some women work for pay or profit the year around; others work only part of the year. There are working women who have worked continuously since leaving school, but there are many others who have worked only periodically: entering, leaving, and re-entering the labor force in response to the perceived demands of child-bearing and child-rearing activities. All of these women could be considered as having the same labor force status. They could all be counted as "in the labor force" for a given enumeration. Accordingly, important dimensions of labor force attachment cannot be inferred from looking only at the labor force status of women at a single point in time.[2] A preliminary step in trying to describe or explain the labor force participation of women is, therefore, to ascertain the variable dimensions of their participation.

Dimensions of Labor Force Attachment

When one considers the notion of primary or career participation as juxtaposed to secondary or non-career participation the following dimensions of labor market activity are distinguishable: continuous vs. non-continuous; year-around vs. temporary; and full-time vs. part-time. Continuous participation is

47

thought of as consecutive participation or labor market
activity which commences after formal school and
continues through the years without long-term
interruptions until retirement age. The continuity of
work experience has been measured as the proportion of
years after leaving school in which one works some
minimum part of the year, i.e., at least half of the
year (see Polachek, 1975; Suter and Miller, 1973).

The continuity of participation is an important
dimension of labor force attachment but, as previously
defined, it does not necessarily tap the nature of
employment within a given year. More particularly, we
do not know whether employment is year-around or
seasonal. This intra-year dimension of labor force
participation is measured by the actual number of weeks
worked per year, with year-around employment commonly
defined as 50 to 52 weeks (see U.S. Bureau of the
Census, 1973).

Finally, the continuity of participation provides
no information on whether employment within a given
year is full-time or part-time. This variable
dimension of intra-year employment is measured by the
number of hours worked per week. Full-time
participation has been defined recently as 40 or more
hours a week, although less stringent definitions are
often used. In 1960 the U.S. Bureau of the Census
defined full-time participation as 35 or more hours a
week, and in 1970 the definition was expanded to
include workers employed 30 or more hours a week.

In summary, three dimensions of labor market
activity have been distinguished which are ignored in
studies of labor force status. These variable
dimensions are: (1) the proportion of years worked
since leaving regular school; (2) the number of weeks
worked per year; and (3) the number of hours worked per
week. The problem now is to incorporate these variable
dimensions of labor force participation into a summary
measure of labor force attachment.

The Measure of Labor Force Attachment

If one had access to "ideal" information, all
three variables could be combined by a simple process:
(step 1) take the total number of weeks worked for all
years since leaving school; (step 2) weight each week
worked by the number of hours worked, i.e., "1" for 40
hours or more, ".8" for 35 to 39, etc.; (step 3) divide

48

by the total number of weeks at risk or since leaving
school. A computing formula for such ideal data would
look something like this:

$$LFA = \Sigma WW/TW$$

where WW is the number of weeks worked by the
respondent since leaving regular school weighted by
hours worked per week; and TW is the total number of
weeks since the respondent left school.

Given departures of available information from
the conceived ideal, the measure of labor force
attachment was revised somewhat. The following formula
was applied to the NLS data on mature women:

$$LFA = \{(A/B)+(C/24)+(D/24)\}50$$

where A is the number of years in which the respondent
worked at least six months between leaving regular
school and 1967; B is the number of years since the
respondent left school and 1967; C is the sum of hours
worked per week between 1967 and 1971 as categorized
into values ranging from 0 to 12^3; and D is the number
of weeks worked per year summary between 1967 and 1971
as categorized into values ranging from 0 to 12^4. A/B
thus reflects the dimension of continuity prior to the
initial survey in 1967, while C and D tap intra-year
dimensions of labor market experience from 1967 to
1971. More complete and technical descriptions of the
LFA measure and the component variables used in
formulation of the LFA measure are given in Table 3.3
and the appendix, but a few general comments are
necessary for an adequate interpretation of the
resulting index.

Note that the continuity of participation (A/B)
yields a maximum value of 1.00. Given the age range of
this sample of women, and the greater propensity for a
re-entry type of participation among mature women, the
influence of recent labor market behavior should not be
allowed to outweigh labor market experience before the
initial survey. The C and D values are each divided by
24 to discount the possible over influence of re-entry
participation after the prime childbearing and
childrearing years. When divided by 24 (a constant
representing twice the maximum possible value), neither
C nor D can realize a value greater than .5 and,
accordingly, C + D cannot exceed a value of 1.00. So
the respondent's recent participation behavior (after
1967) cannot contribute more than 50 percent toward a
maximum LFA score. Stated another way, the maximum
value for recent labor market activity (1.00) can equal
but cannot exceed the maximum value for labor market
activity before 1967 (1.00). In order to obtain a high

49

LFA score, the respondent must have high values for both recent labor force participation <u>and</u> earlier continuity.

The sum of the dimensional values is multiplied by 50 to yield an index which varies from 0 to 100. A zero value represents no significant labor force participation: no years in which the respondent worked at least six months between leaving school and the initial survey in 1967; and no employment between 1967 and 1971. The upper limit of 100 represents consecutive employment during all years between leaving school and the first interview, and 50 to 52 weeks of work per year during 1967 through 1971 with an average of 40 hours or more of work per week. Since the maximum value of 100 is obtained only by respondents with employment values above what are considered maximum (career) in other studies, a value of 80 was decided upon as the quantitative definition of career or primary participation. A complete description of the typology of labor force attachment used in this research is presented in Table 3.1.

Overall, the mean value for A/B (.39) indicates that women 30-44 years of age have worked approximately one-third of the years since leaving school. One-half of all women in this age cohort have worked more than one-third of these years and eleven percent have worked continuously (more than 90 percent of this time). Between 1967 and 1971 roughly one-third of mature women could be found in full-time employment at any given point in time and approximately one-fourth to one-third could be found in year-around jobs. From 1968 to 1971 there was a slight decrease in full-time participation (from 33 to 28 percent), which may reflect the tendency for a shorter work week--less than 40 hours a week--to be considered full-time participation. Indeed, over the same period the proportion of women working year-around increased from 24 percent in 1968 to 32 percent in 1971.

Over 90 percent of mature American women have some measurable labor force experience. The median LFA value for all mature women is 37.5 and the mean is 40.8. However, there is considerable variation in LFA scores among women. The standard deviation in LFA is 29 points. Sixty-one percent of mature women have a summary labor force attachment score below 50, while 30 percent have scores of 60 or above. Hence, the labor force attachment of mature American women is highly variable.

50

TABLE 3.1: WOMEN'S LABOR FORCE ATTACHMENT

Type of Labor Force Attachment	Range of LFA Scores	Mean LFA	Total	Dimensions of LFA		
				Mean of A/B Values	Mean of C Values	Mean of D Values
Career	80 - 100	89	14.0	.91	.42	.44
Strong	60 - 79	69	15.6	.65	.35	.38
Moderate	40 - 59	49	19.2	.38	.29	.30
Sporadic	20 - 39	29	21.0	.29	.14	.15
Casual	1 - 19	10	21.8	.13	.04	.04
None	0	0	8.5	.00	.00	.00
% of Total	0 -100	41	100.0	.39	.21	.22

A Typology of Work Patterns

Five types of labor force attachment are delineated in Table 3.2, each of which is characteristic of an important segment of the population of American women. These five types of attachment along with the category "none" are defined on the basis of the LFA index and represent distinctions which are heuristic but arbitrary (as some will undoubtedly argue). In this regard the twain of quantification and qualification will not be "twain enough" for some tastes and will be "too twain" for others. For their consolation I can only offer as justification my observation that the most intelligible qualities are informed by distinctions of quantity and that quantities are always informed by the meaning (quality) of categorization at some stage of inquiry.

The notion of "career participation" as developed in studies concerning women is that of participation in a manner similar to men. In this sense, career participation is closely related to the notion of "primary participation" the major difference being that the term is applied to working women who participate in a certain manner as well as automatically to working men. More specifically, women distinguished as career participants in the American occupational structure are characterized by continuous, year-around, and full-time employment. The quantitative distinction of career attachment encompasses 14 percent of all mature women and 15.3 percent of those women who have ever experienced labor market activity.

The primary difference between the two highest categories of labor force attachment lies in the dimension of continuity. Women with strong attachment average about one-third less participation in the earlier years than do career women. While women in the second category also average fewer weeks worked per year and fewer hours worked per week, those differences are not as substantial. The same observations can be made about differences between strong and moderate workers. Moderate workers average almost 50 percent less labor force continuity than those with strong attachment, and their participation appears largely to be of the late entry/re-entry variety.

On the other hand, differences between those with moderate attachment and sporadic workers are largely within the two intra-year dimensions. Sporadic workers tend to have some early labor market experience, working almost as continuously as moderate workers during the pre-survey years. They also tend to have some recent experience but, in general, their experience is much more sporadic during the survey years.

Differences between the sporadic and casual categories are sizable for all three dimensions of attachment. Casual workers do evidence some early experience but of a very limited nature, and recent experience also tends to be very light or "casual."

Whether or not one agrees with this particular typology of female labor force attachment, one conclusion is unavoidable. Women differ markedly in their participation patterns. There is an average difference of 20 points in LFA between each of the five categories of attachment as constructed, with standard deviations of no less than 5 points (but not greater than 6.4) within categories. Such an observation can be brought to bear on an important methodological issue.

The point made earlier in the assessment of previous efforts to explain female labor force participation and the rewards derived from participation is that these efforts were handicapped by a methodological error. Table 3.2 illustrates this point. Labor force status during the survey week of 1971 explains only 39 percent of the variation in labor force attachment. To be sure career women and near-career women are represented as in the labor force (95 percent and 83 percent respectively). However, anyone undertaking to explain female labor force participation using the dependent variable of labor force status must also explain the patterns of moderate and sporadic workers (74 percent and 46 percent respectively) as well as more than a few casual workers (17 percent) in one undifferentiated jumble. Indeed of women who were employed during the 1971 survey week, 51 percent had attachment scores below 60.

The Necessity for a Longitudinal, Multidimensional
Measure of Market Work

Direct assessment of the necessity for a longitudinal, multidimensional measure of labor force attachment involves answers to two questions. First, can labor force attachment be inferred from the conventional measure of labor force status? If this is

TABLE 3.2: WOMEN'S LABOR FORCE ATTACHMENT BY LABOR FORCE STATUS, 1971
(PERCENT BY COLUMN)

Type of Labor Force Attachment	In The Labor Force		Not in the Labor Force
	Employed	Seeking Work	
Career	24.8	7.0	1.2
Strong	24.2	14.5	5.2
Moderate	26.1	22.7	10.5
Sporadic	17.8	29.3	24.6
Casual	6.9	21.9	40.1
None	0.1	4.5	18.3
% of Total	54.1	2.2	43.7
Mean LFA	57.7	37.6	20.4

the case, longitudinal measures would be unnecessary. Second, is there such similarity among the component dimensions of labor force attachment at a given point in time that knowledge of one dimension implies knowledge of the other dimensions? If this is the case, a longitudinal measure might be indicated, but such a measure need not be multidimensional.

Question 1: Can dimensions of labor force participation be inferred from the conventional measure of labor force status? "One cannot determine labor force attachment, or more theoretically, the extent of female labor force investment from labor force status" (Maret-Havens, 1977:37). Overall, as noted above, the variable of labor force status during the survey week of 1971 explains less than 40 percent of the variation in labor force attachment. Phrased another way, important dimensions of labor force participation cannot be inferred from the conventional measure of labor force status.

The data presented in Table 3.4 also speak to the necessity for a longitudinal measure of labor force participation. This correlation matrix indicates that there is substantial difference among the component variables of each dimension. In other words, there is considerable change through time. For example, the correlation between c_1 and c_2 is .51 suggesting that among the same respondents, the number of hours worked in 1967 is far from an exact predictor of the number of hours worked in 1968. Similarly, within dimension D, weeks worked in 1967 (d_1) is correlated only .28 with weeks worked in 1968 (d_2). There is a temporal pattern in these observations. In general, the further the variables are removed in time, the lower the correlation. The correlation coefficient between c_2 and c_4 (.36) is significantly lower than the correlation between c_2 and c_3 (.54).

Such findings strongly support the contention that longitudinal measures are necessary. Within dimensions of labor force attachment, changes through time, cannot be inferred from labor force status even for the same respondents in successive years. There is sufficient intradimensional change through time that labor force status should not be used as the primary measure of labor force participation. A synchronic measure simply cannot tap the dynamism of individual work histories. And such dynamism appears to be the rule rather than the exception.

TABLE 3.3: COMPONENT VARIABLES USED IN FORMULATION OF THE LFA MEASURE

Component of LFA Measure	NLS Variable Number	Variable Description
A	VAR 1399	Number of years worked more than six months since leaving regular school and the original survey in 1967
B	VAR 1400	Number of years since leaving regular school and the original survey in 1967
c_1	VAR 0083	Hours worked per week in 1967
c_2	VAR 0863	Hours worked per week in 1968
c_3	VAR 0974	Hours worked per week in 1969
c_4	VAR 2477	Hours worked per week in 1971
d_1	VAR 0170	Weeks worked in 1967
d_2	VAR 0889	Weeks worked in 1968
d_3	VAR 0972	Weeks worked in 1969
d_4	VAR 2154	Weeks worked between 1969 and 1971
$C_{(1971)}$	---	Summary of c_1 through c_4
$D_{(1971)}$	---	Summary of d_1 through d_4

TABLE 3.4: CORRELATION MATRIX OF THE RAW INPUT VARIABLES FOR 1971 LFA

	B	c_1	c_2	c_3	c_4	d_1	d_2	d_3	d_4
A	.40	.17	.08	.13	.03*	.35	.15	.12	.07
B		.01*	-.01*	.00*	-.02*	.04	.02*	.02*	-.04
c_1			.51	.55	.46	.21	.16	.10	.01*
c_2				.54	.36	.15	.21	.12	.02*
c_3					.57	.18	.16	.15	.07
c_4						.12	.11	.16	.19
d_1							.28	.24	.16
d_2								.47	.17
d_3									.36

*Not statistically significant at the .01 level

Question 2: Is there such similarity among the component dimensions of labor force attachment at a given point in time that knowledge of one dimension implies knowledge of the other dimensions? While the intradimensional variables tend to show a moderate correlation, the interdimensional variables (A, c_1, c_2, c_3, c_4, d_1, d_2, d_3, d_4) are, at best, only weakly related. The range of correlations between the c and d variables is .01 to .21. For the A and c variables, the range is .03 to .17. Correlation coefficients between the A and d variables range from .07 to .35. In general, the more removed the variables are in time, the lower the correlation coefficients (a pattern also observed for the intradimension correlations). While c_1 and d_1 are weakly correlated (.21), c_1 and d_4 evidence no relation (.01). Hence, question 2 is also answered in the negative. Information for one dimension does not imply knowledge of the other dimensions. Thus, measures of labor force participation should be based on multidimensions of work experience. Certainly, one dimension of work experience cannot serve as a surrogate for the others. They are far from being interchangeable or mutually predictable.

Overall, the original correlation matrix has a determinate of correlation of .109, which indicates that covariance among the variables is just over 10 percent. There exists considerable difference among the variables both within dimensions through time and among dimensions at a given point in time. Such observations indicate the necessity of both longitudinal and multidimensional measures for women's market work.

Notes
Chapter Three

[1]Previous studies of female labor force participation have been relatively successful in explaining variation at the aggregate level but relatively unsuccessful in explaining women's participation at the individual level. Using cross-sectional data for SMSA's with populations of 250,000 or more, Cain (1966:48,54), for example, was able to explain 69 percent of the variation in the 1950 labor force participation rates of married women and 60 percent of the variation in the 1960 labor force participation rates. However using disaggregated data, Cain (1966:94,107) was not able to explain more than 22

percent of the variation in female labor force participation. Similarly, Bowen and Finegan (1969) were able to explain much more of intercity variation than of variation among women. A recent study using the same NLS data set could account for only 27 percent of the variation in women's labor force participation (see Knutson and Schreiner, 1975:6).

[2]In regard to this point, Bowen and Finegan state (1969:3): Still, the fact that we do not deal as fully with variations in hours worked among different groups of participants as with differences in labor force participation rates means that this study must be regarded as something less than a full-fledged treatment of all dimensions of labor supply.

[3]Number of hours worked per week recoded:

0 = 0 hours
1 = 1-20 hours
2 = 21-39 hours
3 = 40 or more hours

$$C = \Sigma(c_1 + c_2 + c_3 + c_4)$$
c_1 1967
c_2 1968
c_3 1969
c_4 1971

[4]Number of weeks worked per year recoded:

0 = 0 weeks
1 = 1-26 weeks
2 = 27-49 weeks
3 = 50-52 weeks

$$D = \Sigma(d_1 + d_2 + d_3 + d_4)$$
d_1 1967
d_2 1968
d_3 1969
d_4 1971

CHAPTER FOUR

INFLUENCES ON THE WORK PATTERNS OF MATURE WOMEN

The presumption underlying this study is that women with markedly different participation patterns not only experience different rewards but that their participation itself is influenced by different conditions. A comparison of the explanatory power of this study to the explanatory power of previous studies at the individual level provide an empirical basis for this expectation (see summary models in Chapter Five).

At the very least, most would agree that occupational rewards can only be compared for those who have similar participation patterns, such provides methodological justification for the effort to distinguish dissimilar patterns as preliminary to studies of status attainment and mobility. At most the identification of differences will also lead to greater order in identifying the determinants of participation. To this task the remaining pages of Chapter Four are devoted.

For the tabular presentations which follow, the LFA values have been grouped into the categories of labor force attachment described in Table 3.2. Unless commented upon in the text, the reader should assume that the universe is that of all mature women and that missing cases do not affect the distribution of LFA. In those instances where missing values or a restricted universe (i.e., only those currently employed or only those currently married) do change the distributions, the changes are noted.

The tables report breakdowns of female labor force attachment by significant independent variables and are percentaged by column. The tables also report "percent of total," or the percentage which each column or category of the independent variable is of the total, and "mean LFA," or the average LFA value for each column or category of the independent variable. Unless noted, the reader is to assume that there is significant variation among these categorical means of

61

LFA (at the .001 level or beyond). Of course, statistically insignificant results constitute a form of negative finding which may be of interest and importance, and some negative results are discussed in the text.

The subsequent analysis of women's labor force attachment considers three groups of independent variables or "determinants." The next section considers variables which reflect a respondent's situation of origin or formative influence during her adolescence. The second and third sections consider aspects of recruitment. The second looks at conditions of supply. These supply conditions pertain to the personal characteristics and situation of the respondent circa 1967. The third considers the situation of demand as such pertains to characteristics of the respondent's job and to the general labor market. Because the variables are time-lagged we are justified in making inferences of a causal nature i.e., in talking of "determinants" of women's labor force attachment. However, to begin cautiously, we will simply explore variations in observed patterns of labor force attachment as such variations are correlated with a number of social origin and recruitment conditions.

> . . . the questions we are continually raising in one form or another are: how and to what degree do the circumstances of birth condition subsequent status? and, how does status attained (whether by ascription or achievement) at one stage of the life cycle affect the prospects for a subsequent stage (Blau and Duncan, 1967:164)?

Turning to the central questions raised by Blau and Duncan, one important circumstance of birth, an ascriptive status, is that of sex itself. Indeed, Blau and Duncan predicated their study on the fundamental assumption that women would not be represented in the status system of the American occupational hierarchy. Empirically, we have seen that the ascriptive status of sex does not determine participation in the status hierarchy of the American occupational structure, although it remains an important influence. Men are more likely than women to participate in the American occupational structure as a primary status system. In other words, the status of female is associated with much greater variation in attachment to the system of positions and rewards termed "the American occupational structure." A preliminary set of questions applicable

62

to women thus concerns the determinants of their labor force attachment.

Work Patterns and Social Origins: Background Characteristics

How do other circumstances of birth and upbringing affect the labor force attachment of women? Perhaps the most important ascriptive status beside that of sex itself is ethnic status as transliterated into the social construct of "color" or "race." Certain ethnic backgrounds condition life chances to an inordinate degree and such differential opportunities have led some observers to the conclusion of a caste system in the United States based upon "color." To be an American of African ancestry is associated with a distinctive set of expectations, of which low socioeconomic status for both position of origin and position of destination are usual elements.

Is the achievement of low status due to a lack of effort or attachment to the status system? Table 4.1 suggests that, to the contrary, black women are overrepresented in the two highest categories of labor force attachment. Black women are considerably more likely than white women to be primary participants in the American occupational structure. Forty-three percent of black women and 30 percent of other "noncaucasian" women. These findings do not support the conclusion of previous studies that a differential of about 12 percentage points in the labor force participation rates of black and nonblack women are "offset by differences in hours worked by white and Negro women" (Bowen and Finegan, 1969:91; also see Cain, 1966:80-81).

The present results indicate that black women average 10 percent greater labor force attachment than white women, which is only slightly less than the gap in labor force participation rates observed. This difference is, in part, attributable to a greater continuity of participation prior to 1967. However, the gap is also due to significantly higher values for the intra-year dimensions of labor force attachment. Since ethnicity has been identified consistently as a major source of difference or "exception" in other studies of women's participation patterns and the rewards derived from participation, questions pertaining to ethnic differences in the correlates of labor force attachment are systematically explored in

63

TABLE 4.1: WOMEN'S LABOR FORCE ATTACHMENT BY "RACE" (PERCENT BY COLUMN)

Type of Labor Force Attachment	White	Black	Other
Career	13.2	20.0	18.8
Strong	14.8	22.7	11.6
Moderate	19.2	18.7	20.3
Sporadic	21.3	17.9	26.1
Casual	22.6	15.3	20.3
None	9.0	5.4	2.9
% of Total	87.1	11.1	1.9
Mean LFA	39.7	49.5	44.0

64

the last section of this chapter.

Outside of the distinctive expectations associated with caste position, the socioeconomic position or "social class" of a parental family determines, to a significant degree, a child's access to goods and services including health care and educational opportunities. Hence, social origins exert a strong influence on "chances for achieving any other status. . . " (Blau and Duncan, 1967:295). As Blau and Duncan state (1967:207):

> Equality of opportunity is an ideal in the United States, not an accomplished fact. The chances of occupational achievement are limited by the status ascribed to a man as the result of the family into which he was born. Indeed, a stable society is hardly conceivable that does not ascribe to every child a status in some kinship group, which is responsible for rearing and socializing him, and which, therefore, strongly influences his motivation to achieve, his qualifications for achievement, and hence his chances for success.

How, then, do various aspects of the position and structure of the parental family influence a woman's attachment to the American occupational structure?

Occupation of father (or household head) when the respondent was age 15 and the educational attainments of parents are indicators of the socioeconomic status or "social class" of the family of orientation. The amount of formal schooling obtained by parents is also used to indicate the educational climate of the parental home, which Blau and Duncan found to be of great importance in the process of male status attainment.

To begin with a negative finding, the educational attainment of mothers (other than household heads) is not significantly associated with daughters' subsequent labor force participation. The socioeconomic status of family of orientation, as measured by the educational attainment of the household head does exert a moderate influence on daughters' labor force attachment (explaining less than one percent of the total variation). Surprisingly, however, the effect is negative. Table 4.2 reports that respondents coming from families in which the head completed less than 12

65

years of school are more likely than other women to be career participants in the American labor force. Alternatively, women reared in homes with college educated heads are more likely than other women to have no significant labor force participation. Apparently an upper middle class life style during the late 1930's through the early 1950's is not conducive to daughters' strong attachment to the extra familial occupational world.

This conjecture is supported by the findings reported in Table 4.3. Daughters raised in environments associated with professional and managerial occupations for fathers are less likely than other women to be primary participants in the extra-familial occupational world and less likely to be unmarried. Perhaps, given a situation of marital endogamy, women with high socioeconomic origins have better marital options and are selectively recruited into marriage to high status men. In other words, their main process of status attainment may be through marriage. In regard to this process of status attainment for women, there is a significant association between the occupation of father and the occupation of husband for respondents who were married in 1967.

To digress for a moment regarding such a process of "marital mobility" for women (indeed this is the traditional method of determining the social mobility of women), Tables 4.4 and 4.5 delineate the patterns of association between father's occupation and husband's occupation for respondents who were married in 1967. Table 4.4 presents the transition matrix of intergenerational marriage mobility; that is, movements between father's occupation and husband's occupation in 1967. The table percentages, which are computed horizontally or by row, indicate the out-flow from occupational origins indexed by father's occupation to occupational destination indexed by husband's occupation. The column totals in Table 4.4 reflect the percent of women in the various marital destinations. It is evident that the 12 occupational categories were not equal, ranging from 1.2 percent of total married women for farm laborers to approximately 20 percent for craftsmen, and operatives, and roughly 15 percent for professionals, and managers.

Comparing percentages within the same column, generally, the percentages are highest in the major diagonal and decrease with movement away from it, a

TABLE 4.2: WOMEN'S LABOR FORCE ATTACHMENT BY SOCIAL ORIGINS (PERCENT BY COLUMN)

Type of Labor Force Attachment	Education of Father or Household Head					
	5 yrs or less	6 - 8 yrs	9 - 11 yrs	12 yrs	13 - 15 yrs	16 or more yrs
Career	15.3	14.1	17.8	12.9	13.3	12.9
Strong	17.0	14.7	17.2	16.0	10.6	13.5
Moderate	19.3	18.8	17.4	20.4	20.5	15.5
Sporadic	19.8	22.6	19.5	24.2	22.7	20.9
Casual	19.6	21.7	20.2	19.6	27.7	26.2
None	9.0	8.1	7.9	6.9	5.3	11.1
% of Total	20.0	41.7	11.7	16.0	4.8	5.8
Mean LFA	42	40	44	41	39	36

TABLE 4.3: WOMEN'S LABOR FORCE ATTACHMENT BY SOCIAL ORIGINS (PERCENT BY COLUMN)

Type of Labor Force Attachment	Occupation of Father or Household Head											
	Prof.	Mgr.	Cler.	Sales	Craft	Oper.	PHH.	Service	Farm	Farm Lab.	Labor	A.F.
Career	12.4	12.7	14.9	17.5	14.6	13.5	17.7	17.5	13.7	11.9	14.2	19.4
Strong	14.4	14.7	15.7	10.9	14.3	15.1	13.1	21.5	19.0	14.2	16.4	18.3
Moderate	19.3	17.1	16.4	12.5	21.8	18.3	18.7	17.9	20.4	19.6	19.8	19.4
Sporadic	23.7	20.4	26.6	21.5	19.8	23.1	23.2	21.5	19.2	21.0	17.8	19.4
Casual	21.3	25.1	21.6	26.7	22.9	21.6	14.6	15.0	19.5	23.3	23.4	14.0
None	8.9	10.1	4.7	10.9	6.7	8.3	12.6	6.5	8.1	10.0	8.5	9.7
% of Total	5.9	11.7	4.0	3.0	16.1	19.7	2.0	4.9	22.1	2.2	7.6	0.9
Mean LFA	39	38	43	39	41	40	42	47	43	38	42	45

68

TABLE 4.4: TRANSITION MATRIX OF INTERGENERATIONAL MARRIAGE MOBILITY: OUTFLOW PERCENTAGES (% BY ROW)

Father's Occupation	Husband's Occupation												
	Prof.	Mgr.	Cler.	Sales	Craft	Oper.	PHH	Service	Farm	FarmLab	Labor	A.F.	Total
Prof.	40.9	20.7	3.7	8.3	11.2	6.5	-	2.0	3.5	0.6	1.2	1.4	100.0
Mgr.	27.1	22.3	4.2	8.3	15.6	13.3	-	1.5	2.6	0.0	3.3	1.8	100.0
Cler.	22.3	15.1	8.0	6.2	21.7	12.8	-	3.9	6.2	0.0	3.9	0.0	100.0
Sales	26.7	18.2	3.6	11.3	17.0	8.5	-	1.6	4.0	0.0	7.7	1.2	100.0
Craft	16.1	13.4	6.3	8.5	27.3	17.3	-	4.0	2.4	0.1	3.1	1.5	100.0
Oper.	13.7	10.7	6.4	3.4	24.7	26.8	-	4.2	2.4	0.6	6.6	0.6	100.0
PHH	1.6	15.3	6.5	2.4	14.5	33.9	-	3.2	2.4	2.4	14.5	3.2	100.0
Service	18.2	10.4	3.9	5.5	25.3	20.3	-	7.3	2.6	1.0	2.9	2.6	100.0
Farm	11.1	11.4	5.3	2.9	19.1	20.4	-	3.8	14.0	2.2	9.3	0.5	100.0
Farm Lab	1.8	6.1	7.4	0.0	22.1	23.3	-	6.1	3.7	13.5	16.0	0.0	100.0
Labor	9.2	15.4	3.4	2.1	21.5	24.4	-	5.9	2.3	1.6	12.5	1.6	100.0
A.F.	20.0	20.0	1.3	8.0	24.0	1.3	-	0.0	8.0	4.0	9.3	4.0	100.0
Total	17.1	14.1	5.3	5.3	21.2	19.1	-	3.8	5.3	1.2	6.4	1.2	100.0

reflection of the tendency toward marital endogamy within occupational categories. But the marital endogamy of women is by no means entirely consistent. Hence, while 41 percent of married women originating from professional origins are married to professional men, 11 percent of women with professional backgrounds are married to craftsmen. Table 4.5 reports the inflow of female marital partners as recruited from various occupational backgrounds. This table also illuminates the dispersion of husbands from the occupational origins of their wives. The greatest marital endogamy is for farmers who recruit approximately 58 percent of their wives from farm families. On the other hand, professional men are more likely to draw their spouses from managerial, craft, and operative backgrounds than from professional backgrounds. However, considering the proportionate availability of women, and comparing across rows, professional wives are disproportionately likely to have professional backgrounds.

A great deal concerning the "marital mobility" of women has been written and the reader is referred to a subsequent volume (Occupational Mobility in America: Bringing Women In) for a more complete analysis of this process of status attainment. A detailed analysis of the occupational mobility of women as an alternative process of status attainment is also presented in that volume. The major question here is whether women are selectively recruited into one or the other process? To approach this question from a slightly different perspective: Are women from certain social origins more disposed to be married? The answer is yes. Women from white-collar origins are disproportionately likely to be married.

This finding reinforces that possible conclusion that women with high social origins are less likely to have strong labor force attachment. High occupational status for the parental family may not provide an environment conducive to the subsequent occupational striving for daughters. The nexus of norms associated with affluent social origins may prescribe the desirability of traditional sex-role behavior, along with the expectation of feasibility for making a "good marriage" and the security of trusting a husband to provide the economic wants of a wife.

As Blau and Duncan state (1967:296), "The family in which a child grows up serves as a prime source of social as well as economic support."

TABLE 4.5: MARRIAGE MOBILITY: INFLOW PERCENTAGES (% BY COLUMN)

Father's Occupation	Husband's Occupation												
	Prof.	Mgr.	Cler.	Sales	Craft	Oper.	PHH	Service	Farm	FarmLab	Labor	A.F.	Total
Prof.	14.6	8.9	4.3	9.5	3.2	2.1	-	3.2	4.1	3.1	1.1	7.3	6.1
Mgr.	19.5	19.4	9.7	19.1	9.1	8.5	-	4.8	6.1	0.0	6.4	18.8	12.3
Cler.	5.3	4.3	6.1	4.7	4.1	2.7	-	4.1	4.7	0.0	2.4	0.0	4.0
Sales	4.6	3.8	2.0	6.3	2.4	1.3	-	1.3	2.3	0.0	3.6	3.1	3.0
Craft	15.5	15.6	19.6	26.4	21.3	14.9	-	17.5	7.4	1.0	8.1	21.9	16.5
Oper.	15.6	14.8	23.5	12.4	22.8	27.4	-	21.7	8.8	9.4	20.1	10.4	19.5
PHH	0.1	1.6	1.8	0.7	1.0	2.6	-	1.3	0.7	3.1	3.4	4.2	1.5
Service	4.9	3.4	3.4	4.7	5.5	4.9	-	8.9	2.3	4.2	2.1	10.4	4.6
Farm	14.4	17.8	21.9	11.9	20.0	23.6	-	22.3	57.9	42.7	32.1	10.4	22.1
Farm Lab	0.2	0.8	2.7	0.0	2.0	2.4	-	3.2	1.4	22.9	4.9	0.0	2.0
Labor	4.0	8.2	4.7	2.9	7.6	9.5	-	11.8	3.2	10.4	14.6	10.4	7.5
A.F.	1.1	1.3	0.2	1.4	1.0	0.1	-	0.0	1.4	3.1	1.3	3.1	0.9
Total	100.0	100.0	100.0	100.0	100.0	100.0	-	100.0	100.0	100.0	100.0	100.0	100.0

In addition to economic support the family of
orientation provides the child with diverse
forms of social support, which range from
such subtle factors as furnishing thought
patterns and role models and having many
books available at home to such explicit ones
as encouraging children to study and helping
them if they have trouble.

To continue the line of reasoning about differential
familial expectations, we would expect "unconventional
backgrounds" to be associated with women's
"unconventional" pursuits of status attainment outside
the boundaries of matrimony. In this regard, the
disproportionate representation of women with military
backgrounds in the extra-familial career category is of
interest.

Coming from a family in which the mother worked
outside the home during the daughter's adolescence is
also somewhat unconventional for mature women. Table
4.6 indicates that two-thirds of mature women were
raised in circumstances in which the mother did not
work outside the home during the daughter's
adolescence. Of women with working mothers, over one-
third are in the career and near-career categories,
compared to slightly over one-fourth of women whose
mothers did not work.

Blau and Duncan found (1967:359) "that being
reared in a broken family is a handicap for subsequent
status achievement" for males. However, this aspect of
parental family structure does not appear to influence
the overall labor force attachment of women. The
summary chi square between labor force attachment and
persons with whom the respondent lived at age 15 is not
significant at the .001 level nor are mean LFA
variations. However, respondents who live with only
one parent were slightly but significantly more likely
to be in the career category than respondents who lived
with two parents (17 percent of those who lived only
with fathers, and 16 percent of those who lived only
with mothers, compared to 14 percent of those who lived
with mother and father and 12 percent of those who
lived with a parent and step-parent).

These findings regarding the structure of the
parental home reinforce the contention of others about
the importance of role modeling. Although family
structure per se provides little information about the
role models in the family of orientation, some

72

TABLE 4.6:   WOMEN'S LABOR FORCE ATTACHMENT
             BY FAMILY STRUCTURE (PERCENT
             BY COLUMN)

Type of Labor Force Attachment	Did Mother Work?	
	Yes	No
Career	16.5	13.2
Strong	17.8	14.4
Moderate	17.5	19.4
Sporadic	19.4	22.1
Casual	21.7	21.7
None	7.1	9.2
% of Total	33.9	66.1
Mean LFA	44	40

inferences can be drawn. The most obvious variable in regard to roles is whether the mother worked outside the home, and this variable does have a significant impact on daughters' subsequent labor force behavior. In addition, in contradiction to the findings for males, coming from a single parent family (a "broken home") is at the least no handicap for the career status of daughters.

Turning to other aspects of ascription, Blau and Duncan observed (1967:275), "The community in which a man is raised, just as the race or ethnic group into which he is born, defines an ascriptive base that limits his adult occupational chances." Blau and Duncan were concerned with three aspects of community of origin: the urbanization of the community; the region of the community; and migration from the community. First, they found (1967:203-214) that men born in the South ("both white and nonwhite") were "disadvantaged in the struggle for occupational success." Table 4.7 suggests that whatever the disadvantages may be to male status attainment, having attended high school in the South tends to encourage rather than to inhibit the labor force attachment of women. Since region of origin does appear to exert an influence on the subsequent participation patterns of women who have at least some high school, regions are further broken down into states. Women from 11 states and the District of Columbia average labor force participation scores of 45 or more, and with two exceptions these are Southern states.

In regard to community size, Blau and Duncan assert:

The community in which a boy is raised affects his career as an adult, just as the region where he was born does. The socioeconomic structure of the community where a boy grows up probably serves as an ascriptive determinant of his later behavior in a manner somewhat similar to his family origins. The adolescent doubtlessly is more aware of career lines to which he has been exposed in his home town, more interested in jobs for which role models exist in his experience, and better prepared for occupations to which the local school system is oriented. Thus we would expect the occupational structure of the community in which a man was raised to influence his

74

TABLE 4.7: WOMEN'S LABOR FORCE ATTACHMENT BY REGION OF ORIGIN
(PERCENT BY COLUMN)

Type of Labor Force Attachment	Regional Division of High School										Total (of those who attended H.S.)
	New England	Middle Atlantic	East North Central	West North Central	South Atlantic	East South Central	West South Central	Mountain	Pacific	Outside U.S.	
Career	12.5	16.1	11.7	13.1	17.9	14.1	16.8	13.4	14.4	14.2	14.6
Strong	16.8	14.8	16.0	14.4	18.8	15.6	17.7	7.3	13.9	13.0	15.6
Moderate	20.2	16.4	19.5	19.6	18.8	20.8	21.1	25.4	22.5	16.3	19.4
Sporadic	29.3	19.3	23.3	20.8	20.1	20.8	18.2	26.1	18.1	24.9	21.3
Casual	16.8	24.0	20.6	25.7	17.3	21.7	18.4	22.8	26.3	23.7	21.5
None	4.5	9.5	8.8	6.5	7.1	6.9	7.8	4.9	4.8	7.9	7.5
% of Total	5.6	19.6	19.2	9.1	14.4	7.8	9.2	4.2	7.0	3.9	
Mean LFA	42	40	40	39	46	41	45	39	42	39	42

future career--and occupation structures vary, of course, with degree of urbanization (1967:262).

. . . there are differences in occupational opportunities between commercial centers, industrial cities, small towns, rural areas, and farms. The division of labor varies from one type of locality to another, and with it the opportunity structure that affects men's careers (1967:243).

The fact dominating the findings of the last section is that urbanization--of place or origin as well as present residence--promotes occupational success. In terms of a man's career the city is a better place than the country, not only as a place to work, but also as a place to grow up (1967:266).

The findings reported in Table 4.8 support Blau and Duncan's conclusion regarding the status attainment process in that women who pursue careers in the American occupational structure are disproportionately recruited from large cities. However, with one exception, there is little variation among other types of backgrounds with farm backgrounds supplying about the same proportion to the career ranks as other rural backgrounds, towns, and medium size cities. The exception is those with suburban backgrounds. Women with suburban upbringings are less likely than other women to have high levels of labor force attachment and, conversely, more likely to have sporadic and casual patterns of participation. Since women with suburban backgrounds are also more likely to come from families with high SES, the explanation that a nexus of family norms associated with a middle-class life style is not conducive to subsequent occupational striving for daughters outside the traditional confines of females sex-role behavior is further supported. Also of interest, are the observations that women with farm backgrounds are more likely than other women to have strong labor force attachment, while women from rural non-farm areas are most likely to have no labor force attachment.

Early cultural influences as measured by residence at age 15 and region of origin, do exert an influence on women's subsequent labor force behavior, but not uniformally in the ways associated with male status attainment. More specifically, women with farm

76

TABLE 4.8: WOMEN'S LABOR FORCE ATTACHMENT BY COMMUNITY OF ORIGIN (PERCENT BY COLUMN)

Type of Labor Force Attachment	Farm or Ranch	Rural – Non Farm	Town or Small City	Suburb of Large City	City of 25,000 to 100,000	Large City
Career	13.8	13.3	13.8	10.2	13.0	16.4
Strong	19.0	13.5	14.3	10.4	15.3	16.0
Moderate	19.8	20.1	20.3	13.7	16.7	18.9
Sporadic	20.7	18.5	20.8	28.9	21.4	20.4
Casual	18.6	22.7	23.0	28.7	25.0	19.4
None	8.1	12.0	7.8	8.2	8.6	8.9
% of Total	23.8	6.8	31.3	4.5	13.6	20.0
Mean IFA	43	38	40	34	39	43

77

backgrounds average the same LFA as women coming from large cities, although women from large cities are disproportionately represented in the career category, while those with farm backgrounds are more likely to have strong attachment.

Finally, Blau and Duncan (1967:214) observed that having moved out of the region of birth is associated with higher occupational status for males. They state (1967:251), "The data unequivocally show that migrants have more successful careers than men still living in their region of birth." In-so-far as having a career in the American occupational structure can be termed a "more successful career," our data suggest an association between residential stability and career levels of labor force attachment. The findings in Table 4.9 indicate that career women are over-represented among those whose birthplace and current residence are within the same state. However, there are no significant differences in average labor force scores between those who have moved from their region of birth and those who have remained in (or returned to) their region of birth.

As reported in Table 4.10, length of residence is also significantly associated with women's labor force attachment, but again not in the manner expected. Migration does not appear to afford any particular advantages to mature women in terms of their involvement in the occupational structure. Indeed mature women who have lived in the same area all their adult lives (30 years or more) are over-represented in the career ranks compared to the recently mobile.

Work Patterns and Conditions of Supply: Personnel Characteristics

The following analysis focuses upon those factors which reflect, more directly, the abilities and personal characteristics of women as potential workers. The interest here is on what women have to offer on the market and on their personal conditions of employment; in other words, on conditions of supply. This section explores three sets of supply factors:[1] (I) those relating to the ability to work or enabling conditions--i.e., respondent's health and preparation for work; (II) those relating to the necessity to work or precipitating conditions--i.e., health of husband, household resources, number of dependents; and (III) those relating to tastes for employment or facilitating

TABLE 4.9: WOMEN'S LABOR FORCE ATTACHMENT BY BIRTHPLACE IN COMPARISON TO CURRENT RESIDENCE (PERCENT BY COLUMN)

Type of Labor Force Attachment	Birthplace in Comparison to 1967 Residence		
	Same State As Cur Res	Dif. State Same Region	Dif. Region
Career	15.2	12.2	12.2
Strong	15.4	16.1	16.0
Moderate	19.0	21.9	17.6
Sporadic	20.5	20.0	22.8
Casual	21.1	22.8	22.7
None	8.8	6.9	8.8
% of Total	59.5	16.4	24.1
Mean LFA	41.5	40.6	39.2

TABLE 4.10: WOMEN'S LABOR FORCE ATTACHMENT BY LENGTH OF RESIDENCE (PERCENT BY COLUMN)

Type of Labor Force Attachment	Years at Current Residence						
	< 3	3-5	6-9	10-15	16-20	21-29	≥ 30
Career	9.8	11.2	12.7	15.8	14.4	13.1	15.6
Strong	12.0	11.8	15.3	15.2	18.1	19.2	16.3
Moderate	22.2	17.9	15.2	18.8	22.4	22.3	18.1
Sporadic	22.6	27.0	26.7	20.0	19.9	17.6	19.2
Casual	25.2	22.5	20.1	22.1	17.8	18.9	22.8
None	8.3	9.5	9.9	8.1	7.4	9.0	8.0
% of Total	8.8	9.8	9.8	15.8	10.2	9.0	36.5
Mean LFA	37	37	39	42	44	42	42

conditions--i.e., marital and family characteristics including nonmarket activities and husband's attitudes, respondent's attitudes about women's roles and about the job.

Enabling Conditions--
Ability for Market Work

Perhaps the most obvious enabling condition is that of health; whether a woman is physically capable of working. Table 4.11 shows that a respondent's health (as she perceived it in 1967) is indeed a significant condition of labor force attachment. Approximately 85 percent of women between the ages of 30 to 44 report that their health is good or excellent and these women are disproportionately represented in the high LFA categories. Fifty-two percent of career women report excellent health compared to only 41 percent of casual workers, and 92 percent of career women rate their health as excellent or good. Overall, there is a linear relationship between health and labor force attachment; the better the health, the higher the mean LFA scores. Health explains about three percent of the variation in women's labor force attachment.

Education for work is another important enabling condition for employment, as many can testify who have attempted to gain employment without the requisite education or training. Education does not ensure employment but, increasingly, certain levels of formal schooling have become entrance requirements for most jobs. As Blau and Duncan state (1967:235):

Education is, of course, not simply technical preparation for adulthood but becomes behavior that is culturally prescribed regardless of whether it is needed for the performance of occupational roles. Thus high-school graduation is coming to be a cultural norm to which most members of our society are expected to conform, as illustrated by the recent concern with high-school dropouts.

Education and training (other than on-the-job training) are also important as indications of "taste" for work and human capital investment. Such is the interpretation used by many economists. For example, Bowen and Finegan (1969:20) assume a positive

81

TABLE 4.11: WOMEN'S LABOR FORCE ATTACHMENT BY ABILITY TO WORK
(PERCENT BY COLUMN)

| Type of Labor Force Attachment | Excellent | Health in 1967 | | Poor |
		Good	Fair	
Career	16.3	13.8	9.1	3.6
Strong	16.2	16.3	12.2	10.2
Moderate	19.2	19.2	18.4	11.8
Sporadic	20.9	21.4	21.7	17.1
Casual	20.3	22.0	25.9	29.9
None	7.0	7.3	12.7	27.3
% of Total	44.4	40.8	12.0	2.8
Mean LFA	43	41	34	24

association between education and "tastes for market work per se."

Generally, education increases the probability of finding work and also increases a person's access to more interesting and more pleasant jobs. Hence, Bowen and Finegan (1969:53) suggest "the opportunity cost of staying out of the labor market is greater for a person with considerable education than for a person with relatively little education." They maintain that this should be true especially for persons with a genuine choice concerning labor force status (other than prime-age males).

The amount of formal schooling has been related to the labor force participation of women in every major study to date. Hence, any other finding would have been surprising indeed. Table 4.12 reports the usual significant association between formal education and employment. There is, moreover, the usual linear relationship between years of school completed and participation scores. The mean LFA rate increases as educational attainment increases. However, the relationship is fairly flat at the middle levels of educational attainment. The difference in average participation scores for women having six to eight years of schooling and those having some college is only four points. The overall spread of 16 points is, in large part, accounted for by two sizable differences: (1) between women having five or less years of school and those having six to eight and (2) between women having some college and those having four years or more.

The first jump in the participation scores of women is similar to the jump in participation rates for males (see Figure 4.1) and, as Bowen and Finegan (1969:73) suggest "is probably in large measure a testament to the importance of achieving functional literacy." Returning to Table 4.12, one can see, however, that the sizable differential in LFA means between the lowest and second educational levels is not accounted for by differences in the career and strong categories. Twenty-two percent of women with five or less years of school have participation scores of 60 and above compared to 25 percent of women with six to eight years of school. Indeed, there is relatively little variation in the strong category among educational levels, with proportionate differences of only three percentage points across all educational levels. This finding suggests that lower opportunity

TABLE 4.12: WOMEN'S LABOR FORCE ATTACHMENT BY PREPARATION FOR WORK (PERCENT BY COLUMN)

Type of Labor Force Attachment	Years of Formal School Completed					
	5 yrs. or less	6-8 yrs	9-11 yrs	12 yrs	13-15 yrs	16 or more
Career	7.5	11.4	12.6	14.0	15.7	23.9
Strong	14.7	14.1	14.7	16.2	16.7	17.8
Moderate	13.6	20.1	22.7	19.0	16.9	13.2
Sporadic	17.2	21.1	21.3	22.0	20.1	17.6
Casual	25.2	21.3	21.4	22.0	23.7	19.3
None	21.9	12.0	7.4	6.9	6.8	8.2
% of Total	3.2	12.7	24.6	41.5	10.0	8.0
Mean LFA	31	38	41	42	42	47

costs for women with relatively little schooling may be offset for many (about one-quarter of them) by other conditions--most likely by precipitating conditions. In this regard, there is a significant association between educational attainment and whether a woman would work if economically unnecessary. And, the lower the educational attainment the lower the proportion of women who say they would work if they did not need the money to cover their needs (only 42 percent of women with less than six years of school say they work compared to 72 percent of women with 16 or more years of school).

The difference between the two lower educational groups is explained in large part by the higher percentage of women with less than six years of school having no significant labor force attachment. It is difficult to explain this finding in terms of differential tastes for employment between the two groups as it is to reconcile it with a difference in functional literacy since we have observed similar distributions for the higher LFA categories. Given previous reports of strong relationship between education and health (see for example Bowen and Finegan, 1969), an explanation was sought in differential health problems. Women with less than six years of school were found to have a high frequency of poor health, and this disabling condition coupled, perhaps, with the extra difficulties of finding work are enough to depress labor force attachment despite precipitating conditions such as low family income.

Juxtaposed to the explanation for the gap between the two lowest educational groups, the jump in labor force attachment between women with some college and women with 16 or more years of school is accounted for primarily by a difference in career participation. There is a difference of only three percentage points between the groups at participation levels below 20, while there is a difference of over nine points at levels above 59, most of which occurs in the career category. Hence, it is more plausible to assume that the completion of at least one college degree does reflect some commitment or "taste" for work and/or high opportunity costs for casual labor force attachment. More than 40 percent of women who completed 16 years of school have labor force participation scores above 59 and nearly one-quarter of these women are career participants in the American occupational structure. This finding has important implications.

A higher proportion of women are completing 16 years of school now than at the time when our women were college age. In 1970, 8.1 percent of women age 25 and over had completed 16 or more years of school, compared to 5.8 percent in 1960 and 5.0 percent in 1950 (U.S. Bureau of the Census, U.S. Summary, Section 1, table 75). Figures for 1970 indicated that 32 percent of women in the ages of 18-24 were enrolled in school, compared to 23 percent in 1960 and 18 percent in 1950 (U.S. Bureau of the Census, U.S. Summary, Section 1, table 73). In other words, the population of women at risk for such career-type participation has been increasing. And, on the basis of our findings, we predict that as these women reach the age of our respondents, a higher proportion of American women will be career members of the labor force.

Although women and men evidence a similar <u>pattern</u> of participation by educational levels, their participation is not the same. More explicitly, the overall attachment rate for mature women who have completed at least four years of college is 47 compared to a participation rate of 98 for similarly educated males. Figure 4.1 also indicates that there is a greater increment in labor force participation explained by "functional literacy" for males than there is for females. The increase in 1970 participation rates between men having less than five years of school is over 13 points, compared to an increase in women's LFA scores of 18 points.

Accordingly, opportunity costs for women may not be the same as for similarly educated males, i.e., males with the same amount of formal education. To put the matter more simply, the quantity of education or years of school completed by men and women cannot be assumed to measure the same qualities for employment as perceived by employers at this point in time. For this reason, education below a college degree is conceptualized as enabling rather than as facilitating women's employment. Indeed Bowen and Finegan (1969:58) appear to conclude with this view of education. They state, "In our view, the main reason a prime-age male's probability of being in the labor force rises with his educational attainment is simply that educational attainment and the ability to find and hold a job are related."

On the other hand, Figure 4.1 denotes that completion of at least one college degree is associated with a greater rise in participation scores for women

86

FIGURE 4.1: LABOR FORCE PARTICIPATION BY EDUCATIONAL ATTAINMENT AND SEX

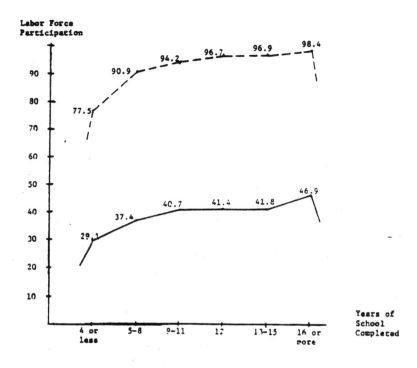

than for men. This finding also has interesting implications for conventional wisdom regarding women's involvement in extra-familial careers is the (unfortunate) lack of involvement in "more normal" pursuits, i.e., having babies. Such misfortune is often attributed to incapacities, i.e., subfecundity. There is a significant association between educational attainment and children, and the relation is negative. More relevant to the line of reasoning outlined here, women with 16 or more years of schooling are disproportionately represented in the category of women who have no children. So, unless an inability to have children was discovered while respondents were still in school or unless higher education engenders an inability to reproduce, one cannot presume causality between not being able to have children and preparing for a career in consolation. To the contrary, the causal nexus can be reversed--those women who prepare for a career are more likely not to have children because of their increased options. (The standard deviation in LFA is higher for women with 16 or more years of school).

To summarize the findings for educational attainment, the correlation ratio of only .009 indicates that years of school completed does not explain very much of the total variation in labor force attachment (less than 1 percent). However, this summary statistic conceals some interesting and important differences among women. Women with under six years of formal schooling are concentrated in the lowest participation levels (47 percent have scores of less than 20), while women with 16 or more years of school are highly over-represented in the career category. Preliminary investigation of these results suggests that the very low participation scores for women with little formal schooling can be explained by poor health, while the high scores for women with college educations can be considered to reflect a taste for non-familial activities. For further substantiation of this conclusion, the reader is referred to the analysis of facilitating conditions (pages 107-112) where the interrelations between education and role attitudes are explored. Education appears more directly related to a variety of facilitating conditions than to labor force attachment per se.

Another variable reflecting preparation for work, which is more strongly related to women's labor force attachment, is that of training other than regular

school. This research indicates that taking a
vocational or commercial curriculum in the formal
educational system (high school) is not significantly
associated with labor force attachment for women; nor
is the sort of skill training involved in high school
typing and/or shorthand courses significantly
associated with subsequent labor force activity. But
technical, commercial or vocational training in
addition to regular school explains more of the
variation in labor force attachment than years of
school completed. Since this variable does not include
on-the-job training, it can be considered a clear
indication of preparation for work and investment on
the part of the respondent. The results are presented
in Table 4.13. Approximately one-third of career women
have some training in addition to formal school
compared to about one-fourth of all mature women.

        The final enabling condition considered is that
of residence in 1967. There is known contamination
between type of area of residence and what are thought
of as "demand" factors, for there is a well-known
association between job opportunities and urbanness.
The observation that job opportunities are better in
cities than in small towns and rural areas is
widespread and for that reason it is considered to be a
condition of supply. A potential worker might not know
which cities currently offer the best prospects of
employment--but most workers, particularly non-farm
female workers, could be expected to know that
prospects for employment are better in urbanized areas.
Indeed, such knowledge on the part of job seekers is
often given to explain the migration from rural areas.
Hence, respondents who choose to live outside of high-
demand areas are limiting their own potential supply of
labor.

        The findings reported in Table 4.14 show, as
expected, that women who live in highly urbanized areas
have greater labor force attachment. What is
unexpected is the relatively slight variation between
women living outside of the central cities. The
difference between those living outside central cities
in an SMSA and those living in areas of relatively low
urbanization is quite small. Moreover, the higher
labor force attachment for women living in central
cities appears to be explained by the disproportionate
representation of these women in the career category
alone. That career women live close to their jobs is
the most plausible explanation. While there has been a
recent trend for businesses and other major employers

TABLE 4.13: WOMEN'S LABOR FORCE ATTACHMENT BY
PREPARATION FOR WORK (PERCENT BY
COLUMN)

Type of Labor Force Attachment	Training Other Than Regular School?	
	Yes	No
Career	18.3	12.6
Strong	17.5	15.0
Moderate	21.3	18.5
Sporadic	20.5	21.1
Casual	16.9	23.3
None	5.5	9.4
% of Total	24.5	75.5
Mean LFA	47	39

(i.e., government) to move outside central cities, that movement is quite recent. Thirty-eight percent of career women live in central cities compared to 28 percent of all mature women. On the other hand, 42 percent of women with no labor force attachment live outside of SMSA's, which is somewhat higher than the sample percentage of 38 percent. In regard to residence choices, career women are similar to career men--they live where the jobs are. Career women are more likely than other women to live in central cities.

However, the findings reported in Table 4.15 indicate that the relationship between labor force attachment and degree of urbanization is by no means linear. Career women are disproportionately concentrated in urbanized areas, but not in the most urbanized.of areas. Here we may, more clearly, be running into problems of demand. As suggested earlier, one could expect urban areas to offer more employment opportunities than rural areas, but differences among particular urban areas and by degree of urbanization are far from obvious. The observation that the most highly urbanized areas contribute proportionately about the same percentage of women to the non-attached ranks as the rural areas is unexplored as is the disproportionate over-representation in the near-career category of women in small urban places of less than 10,000 inhabitants.

To summarize the enabling conditions associated with the labor force attachment of mature American women, career women tend more than other women to: (1) report excellent health; (2) have completed 16 years of formal schooling; (3) have training other than regular school; and (4) be living in the central city of an SMSA and in an urbanized area of greater than one million but less than three million inhabitants.

Precipitating Conditions-- Necessity for Market Work

Given the possibility of employment the next set of questions pertain to the conditions which generate costs for staying out of the labor force. We have already begun to investigate some of these conditions. Good health for women whose presence in the home is not (or no longer) required for the care of children might mean a surplus of energies more fruitfully expended in the labor force. High educational attainment and/or other preparation for employment certainly increase

TABLE 4.14: WOMEN'S LABOR FORCE ATTACHMENT BY RESIDENCE IN (PERCENT BY COLUMN)

Type of Labor Force Attachment	In SMSA		Not in SMSA
	Central City	Not Central City	
Career	19.4	12.6	11.4
Strong	15.7	15.5	15.7
Moderate	18.1	18.2	20.7
Sporadic	18.5	22.6	21.3
Casual	20.8	23.0	21.3
None	7.4	8.1	9.6
% of Total	27.8	34.6	37.6
Mean LFA	44	40	39

TABLE 4.15: WOMEN'S LABOR FORCE ATTACHMENT BY SIZE OF COMMUNITY IN 1967 (PERCENT BY COLUMN)

Type of Labor Force Attachment	Urbanized Areas				Urban Places			Rural Areas
	3,000,000 or more	1,000,000-2,999,999	250,000-999,999	Under 250,000	25,000	24,999	9,999	
Career	16.3	20.7	17.6	14.6	14.8	10.1	13.2	10.3
Strong	13.9	17.9	15.7	17.5	15.0	17.5	19.4	14.4
Moderate	18.1	17.0	18.0	18.9	18.4	21.0	19.7	20.4
Sporadic	18.0	19.0	22.4	18.8	25.9	19.0	20.1	22.9
Casual	23.9	18.4	19.6	22.1	19.4	23.8	21.3	22.4
None	9.8	7.0	6.7	8.1	6.5	8.6	6.2	9.6
% of Total	16.4	9.1	13.2	10.5	3.5	4.7	7.0	35.6
Mean LFA	41	46	44	42	42	40	42	38

opportunity costs for staying home as does living in an area of plentiful opportunities for paid employment. What then are the more negative aspects of a person's situation which might force or "precipitate" working outside the home? The most obvious is the need for money or what is usually termed economic necessity.

Necessity, or what comprises necessity, is not so obvious. What might be considered a necessity by some, for example money to pay for children's college education, would not be considered a necessity by all. Moreover, while need may be the mother of inventions, invention is also the progenitor of need. So a middle-class life style might require a new car, the latest in stereo equipment, and other newly invented (or "improved") consumer durables. In short, above some minimal subsistence level, necessity is arbitrary indeed, and "subjective necessity" may well be the most precipitous of necessities.

In the 1967 survey, all respondents who were employed or looking for work were asked the following question: "If, by some chance, you (and your husband) were to get enough money to live comfortably without working, do you think you would work anyway?" Responses to this question are reported in Table 4.16. Working women who give affirmative responses to this question can be considered as having a taste for economic activity. For working women who respond to this question in the negative, their situation might be interpreted as one in which a "distaste" for paid employment is overcome by the necessity for income.

Such subjective necessity accounts for the labor force participation of 36 percent of all mature women in the labor force in 1967. However, necessity does not explain work motivation for the overwhelming majority of career women. Only one-fourth (27 percent) of the career women report that they would not work compared to 53 percent of the casual workers and 42 percent of sporadic workers. For career women, then, the taste for market activity appears to be a significant and important work motive. For other classes of workers, however, a distaste for their economic circumstances without working (or subjective necessity) appears to be a more important motivation.

Noting that about 85 percent of our sample of women were married with spouse present in 1967 (the investigation of marital status and labor force attachment follows on pages 105-109), what can be said

TABLE 4.16: WOMEN'S LABOR FORCE ATTACHMENT BY ECONOMIC NECESSITY: WORK MOTIVATION IN 1967 (PERCENT BY COLUMN)

Type of Labor Force Attachment	Would Work if Money Were Unnecessary?			Total (of those employed)
	Yes	Undecided	No	
Career	33.2	28.3	22.0	28.9
Strong	29.4	23.2	29.7	29.2
Moderate	25.4	29.5	30.8	27.6
Sporadic	10.3	16.0	13.8	11.8
Casual	1.7	3.0	3.7	2.5
None				
% of Total	59.4	4.5	36.1	
Mean LFA	66	62	60	64

95

about more objective indications of need for those who are married? Having a spouse who cannot work or who has "inadequate" income to support household dependents could clearly precipitate a wife's labor market activity.

Looking first at husband's health, a dichotomized variable of whether or not health prevents husbands' work showed <u>no</u> significant association with the labor force attachment of wives. Turning now to a direct look at household resources as indicative of the need-for-income for married women, the following variables are considered: income of husband, number of dependents, and a variable called "per capita family income," which is total family income minus the wife's income divided by the number of family dependents.

The traditional economic theory of household behavior suggests that "the wife's freedom from the labor market is a normal good, the demand for which can be expected to rise with family income" (Bowen and Finegan, 1969:132). Therefore, the expectation is that the labor force participation of wives should vary inversely with the amount of other family income, the primary component of which is husband's income (Bowen and Finegan, 1969:132). Husband's income in 1966 is significantly associated with the labor force attachment of married women and the overall association is negative (-.05). However, this variable explains relatively little of the overall labor force attachment of wives--only three percent of the variation. Moreover, we did <u>not</u> find the pronounced inverse relationship which <u>was</u> expected. To the contrary, as reported in Table 4.17, there is a linear <u>increase</u> in participation scores among wives until one <u>reaches</u> the two most affluent categories. There is a slight decrease in the average participation of wives in the second highest income category. The sizable dip, which is responsible for the overall weak inverse relationship, occurs in the labor force attachment of "affluent" wives who average 12.4 points below the scores of women married to middle income men ($5,000-$6,999). Women married to affluent husbands (earning $10,000 or more a year in 1966) are more likely than other wives to have casual or no labor force attachment, reflecting, perhaps, a "taste for leisure" or unpaid volunteer activities or activities supportive of the husband's career. Wives with very low income spouses (under $500) are also likely to have low attachment scores in the range of 20 to 39, i.e., sporadic labor force participation. Women married to men with incomes greater than $500 but less than $5,000 are concentrated in the moderate attachment category.

Once again, the strong and career attachment of married women cannot be explained by precipitous economic necessity as objectively defined by marriage to a spouse with very low income in 1966. However, the sizable under-representation of women with high-income spouses in the moderate, strong, and career categories is also of interest. In an attempt to explain this distaste for extra-familial labor outside the conventional argument of the family tax effect (see for example, Bowen and Finegan, 1969:133-138), we looked for a relationship which might vivify the traditional theory of household behavior. We did find a significant association between husbands' income and attitudes toward wives working outside the home. More to the point, high earning husbands were most often perceived as being opposed to their wives' labor market activity. Over one-half (54 percent) of high income husbands are opposed to a wife's work outside the home; a significantly higher proportion than any other income category. Such gives rise to several speculations, three of which are mentioned here. The first is that of the wife's freedom from the labor market is considered "a normal good" by those who can afford a middle-class life style without any monetary contribution by the wife. It is also possible that those women who most desire freedom from labor market activities are more likely to marry and remain married to men who can provide such circumstances. Finally, the substitution effect of replacing the wife's services in the home may be higher for families in which the husband's occupation is furthered by the wife's home activities.

A stronger relationship exists between the labor force attachment of women and number of household dependents (the correlation ratio is .10), but the relationship is inverse. The findings reported in Table 4.18 indicate that a large number of household dependents (excluding the respondent and husband) is, overall, an important deterrent to women's labor force attachment. There is a consistent and sizable decrease in average participation scores as number of dependents increases to five or more.

The most impressive dip is not, as one might suppose, between women without dependents and those with one but, rather, between women with one dependent and those with two dependents. Women with two

TABLE 4.17: WOMEN'S LABOR FORCE ATTACHMENT BY ECONOMIC NECESSITY: HOUSEHOLD RESOURCES (PERCENT BY COLUMN)

Type of Labor Force Attachment	Husbands Income in 1966							Total (of married)
	Less Than $500	$500-$1,499	$1,500-$2,999	$3,000-$4,999	$5,000-$6,999	$7,000-$9,999	$10,000 or More	
Career	9.4	9.0	10.3	10.7	13.3	11.0	6.2	10.1
Strong	14.4	15.8	18.2	19.5	18.1	14.5	10.2	14.9
Moderate	17.6	26.0	24.3	25.7	21.4	20.4	13.8	19.6
Sporadic	26.0	17.5	16.7	17.7	20.8	24.1	25.2	22.9
Casual	22.7	24.9	19.9	17.4	20.4	22.5	33.1	23.8
None	9.9	6.8	10.6	9.0	6.1	7.5	11.5	8.7
% of Total	15.7	2.0	3.8	10.1	19.4	27.7	21.2	
Mean LFA	36	38	40	43	43	39	29	38

TABLE 4.18: WOMEN'S LABOR FORCE ATTACHMENT BY ECONOMIC NECESSITY: RESOURCE DEPENDENTS (PERCENT BY COLUMN)

Type of Labor Force Attachment	Number of Dependents in 1967					
	0	1	2	3	4	5 or more
Career	37.5	22.0	11.6	6.4	5.2	6.4
Strong	19.5	20.3	17.2	13.9	13.1	9.8
Moderate	13.5	21.2	19.8	22.7	17.3	18.6
Sporadic	13.1	16.0	21.9	23.1	26.0	24.1
Casual	10.2	14.2	21.2	24.6	29.0	30.2
None	6.3	6.3	8.3	9.2	9.5	11.0
% of Total	14.0	13.5	24.8	20.1	13.5	14.1
Mean LFA	59	50	40	35	32	31

dependents average ten percent lower labor force
attachment than those with one. A dip of almost 5
points occurs between two and three dependents;
thereafter the decrease lessens. A more detailed
breakdown by number of dependents revealed a slight
increase of one point in average labor force attachment
from six to seven dependents and, then, a continued
decrease of about eight points from seven to nine or
more dependents. Women with six and seven dependents
are also somewhat more likely than women with three
dependents to be found in the career category. The
difference is not large (not more than 2 percent) but
does, nevertheless, constitute a departure from the
overall patterns. A general distaste for market work
and/or household constraints against working for women
with a large number of dependents apparently does not
pertain to all such women. A suspicion that this
departure may be due to the differential household
structures for black women is investigated later.
Meanwhile, we conclude that having a large number of
dependents in the household does not, in general,
precipitate high degrees of labor force attachment.

There is overall, decreasing representation in
the participation levels of 60 and above with an
increase in dependents, and increasing representation
in the sporadic, casual, and none categories as number
of dependents increases. Forty-two percent of women
with one dependent have participation scores which
qualify them as strong and career participants
contrasted with 16 percent representation for women
with five or more dependents. On the other hand, 43
percent of women with five or more dependents have
casual or no participation compared to 20 percent of
women with one dependent. Hence, the economics of
having many dependents might be said to "precipitate"
some labor force activity, but such does not appear to
precipitate very strong attachment to the labor force.

In an effort to combine what are usually thought
of as the precipitating conditons of having many
dependents plus low household resources, a new variable
was created which pertains to the economic
circumstances of married respondents. This measure,
"per capita family income," is similar to the variable
used by Bowen and Finegan (1969:132-147) and includes
in the numerator all family income earned by family
members, other than the wife, as well as property
income. However, it differs from previous measures in
that family income is divided by the number of resource
dependents including the husband and respondent. The

results reported in Table 4.19 thus pertain to per capita family resources; or resources taking into account resource demands.

Again, the findings do not support the generalized expectation that married women's labor force attachment is precipitated by economic necessity. "The expected direction of effect is clear-cut: other things equal, the expected labor force participation rate should vary inversely with the amount of other family income" (Bowen and Finegan, 1969:132). Per capita income resources (without the respondent's contribution) have a positive impact on the labor force attachment of wives. In other words, the greater the resources, the greater the labor force attachment of married women who worked in 1966! Economic necessity does not explain the labor force attachment of many married women, most particularly of women who are career participants in the American occupational structure.

Evidently, previous findings of a negative association between economic resources and women's labor force participation were due, in large part, to the representation of moderate, sporadic and casual workers in the labor force participation rates. The labor force participation of these women does appear to be precipitated by a variety of disadvantageous economic circumstances, including low per capita household resources.

In concluding this analysis of precipitating conditons for female labor force attachment, such conditions as are reflected in subjective necessity and low income-adequacy (low per capita income) for married women do not appear to generate more than casual and sporadic attachment to the labor force. On the other hand, married women with high-income husbands are also significantly under-represented in the career ranks, which suggests that other conditions of marriage and personal life may pose a conflict for strong labor force attachment. It is to a consideration of these facilitating conditions that we turn next.

One of the well-known characteristics of female labor force participation is that women tend to be more participation prone at certain ages (see page 16). Participation rates are high for young women 18-24 and for middle-age women 45-54. They are quite low for women 25 to 34. The major reason suggested for this intervening dip in labor force participation is that

TABLE 4.19: WOMEN'S LABOR FORCE ATTACHMENT BY ECONOMIC NECESSITY: PER CAPITA FAMILY RESOURCES (PERCENT BY COLUMN)

Type of Labor Force Attachment	Other Per Capita Family Income in 1966 (Married Women)							Total (of those married)
	less than $1,000	$1,000-$1,499	$1,500-$1,999	$2,000-$2,999	$3,000-$3,999	$4,000-$5,999	$6,000 or more	
Career	8.7	7.5	10.4	11.4	13.3	18.0	18.8	10.0
Strong	14.7	17.0	14.4	12.8	19.6	13.3	20.3	14.6
Moderate	22.3	18.7	22.8	19.1	13.6	15.4	14.3	19.5
Sporadic	21.9	24.6	22.8	23.0	19.6	19.1	19.5	22.8
Casual	23.6	23.1	24.1	24.3	23.5	25.5	20.3	24.0
None	8.8	9.2	5.5	9.4	10.3	8.8	6.8	9.0
% of Total	17.1	17.0	15.1	18.5	7.2	4.0	1.4	
Mean LFA	37	37	39	38	40	41	45	37

102

tastes for homemaking and childrearing activities outweigh the desire for employment outside the home. Age differences are also said to reflect differences in experience and expectations as well as differential stages in the life-cycle. The older women in this sample were reaching maturity during the depressed 1930's, while the younger women approached maturity during the prosperous 1950's--a considerable difference in experiences. Finally, age is associated with health (see U.S. Department of Labor, 1970:30); an increase of health problems for older women could be expected to depress their labor force participation.

Hence, for several reasons, one could expect age "to make a difference." Certainly, labor force participation rates vary by age cohort for women the approximate ages of our sample. The labor force participation rates in 1970 for mature women by five-year cohorts are:

30-34	44.2
35-39	48.3
40-44	52.1

There is a steady increase in labor force participation rates by age. However, contrary to expectation, the association between LFA categories and age is not significant (at .001).

Age is <u>not</u> significantly related to the summary labor force attachment of mature women. The total variation in mean LFA is less than 3.0 among the three cohorts, and not one of the category means differs by as much as 1.5 from the grand mean. This finding is of methodological and substantive interest.

Although the measure was constructed to minimize differentials due to differences in labor force exposure, the focus was on the mathematical equalization of early and recent labor force experience. Since recent experience spans a period of only five and one-half years (1966 to 1971) and is weighted equally with early history spanning, in most cases, a considerably longer time of possible experience since leaving school, the fear was that the results would still be contaminated by the disproportionate effects of recent labor force experience. As suggested by the labor force participation rates given above, the recent experience of the older cohort of women (40-44) is significantly higher than for the youngest cohort (30-34). Dimension

"D" breaks down by the three age cohorts as follows: .20, .22, .24. Given a range of .00 to .50 for this dimension, the observed variation by age is not overwhelming, although it is statistically significant. However, given no age differences on dimension "AB" the greater re-entry type of participation for older women was not sufficient to markedly change the LFA scores.

Substantively, the only reasons to expect differences in the overall labor force behavior of women by age cohorts would be (a) substantial differences in health, which would act to depress the labor force attachment of older women and/or (b) differences in norms regarding labor market behavior. The negative findings are, therefore, of some interest. Although older women do tend to be more participation prone at a given point in time, older women do not differ significantly from younger women in the overall extent or type of their labor force attachment. More specifically, older women in this sample are neither more nor less likely than women ten years junior to be career participants in the American occupational structure. To know the age of women as such reflects stages in the life-cycle that may be predictive of participation rates, but it is not predictive of the type of labor force attachment. Interpreted in a theoretical context, age is not a sufficient indication of role investment.

Facilitating Conditions--
Tastes for Market Work

This section on facilitating conditions is concerned with the circumstances and values (orientations) of respondents most likely to facilitate or, alternatively, to impede their commitment to labor market activity. Perhaps, the most important set of such conditions has to do with familial values and commitments. An emphasis on familial values can be expected to conflict with women's participation in extra-familial economic activities (see Havens and Gibbs, 1975). As Oppenheimer (1970:52) and others have observed, the negative attitudes toward women working outside the home almost always entail expressions that such work conflicts with a woman's place in the home. Familial values emphasize (1) the familial goals of marriage, home, and children and (2) the familial roles of wife-mother-homemaker. Hence, the theoretical expectation is that the greater women's commitment to familial roles and values, the less their attachment to the labor force.

Phrased another way, the expectation is that investment in traditional sex-role behavior for women will depress their labor force attachment. Interpreted in this light, the negative findings for age would suggest that age cannot be used as a general proxy for sex-role investment for all women. Nor need have we for such a proxy. Such investment can be assessed more directly by looking at marital investment, child investment, and respondents' attitudes toward women's place.

Marriage might be said to represent the first stage of such an investment in the traditional sex-role behavior of wife-mother-homemaker. Certainly, marriage as an institution is variable, but as Safilios-Rothschild (1974:109) has observed, the expectation of marriage is predominantly the expectation that a woman will also be a mother and a homemaker, with primary if not sole investment in these roles.

Given traditional sex-role expectations, marriage can hence be suggested as reflecting a distaste for work outside the home. Certainly, economists make a strong case for marriage as an inducement to male labor force participation. As Bowen and Finegan state (1969:43):

> According to the tastes interpretation, it is the increased financial responsibilities accompanying marriage which cause a greater taste for income, and thus more labor force participation, on the part of married men. Furthermore, it can be argued that marriage affects a man's taste for work directly by increasing the psychic costs of nonparticipation. In our society, both the wife and her friends are likely to look on the husband who is out of the labor force with something akin to scorn, whereas the man without immediate family responsibilities who wants to loaf every now and then can do so relatively free of such nagging. Marital status may also serve as a pure proxy for tastes for market work in that men with a pronounced preference for the free and easy life may for that reason choose not to marry (or not to stay married).

105

Each of the reasons cited above to expect the greater labor force attachment of married men, can be transliterated to expect the lower labor force attachment of married women. First, decreased financial responsibilities for women who marry would decrease the taste for money income. Second, increased responsibilities inside the home should cause less labor force participation for married women. Third, it can be argued that marriage affects a woman's taste for work directly by increasing the psychic costs of participation. "In our society," both the husband and others are likely to look upon the wife's outside employment as a selfish undertaking unless such employment is due to financial necessity (which is taken as a "sign of masculine failure"). Whereas the woman without a husband who wants to pursue a career in the labor force can do so relatively free of "such nagging." Finally, marital status may serve as a "pure proxy for tastes for market work" in that women with a pronounced preference for the responsibilities of a non-familial career "may for that reason choose not to marry" (or not to stay married).

Recent evidence indicates that expectations associated with the wife-mother-homemaker role are associated with negative attitudes toward the long-term employment of women outside the home. Oppenheimer (1970:52) states: "The most consistently important factor determining negative attitudes toward the employment of married women is the conviction that it conflicts with a woman's home responsibilities." Indeed, Oppenheimer finds "no evidence that this conviction has diminished much throughout the years." The employment of women outside the home has been taken as a "challenge to the traditional division of labor" (Blood, in Nye and Hoffman, 1963:285) and as "a sign of masculine failure" (Smuts, 1959:122). Epstein (1970:22-24) also comments on the perceived conflict between definition of "the nature of women" and primary participation of women in extra-familial economic activities:

> The woman who takes her work seriously--the career woman--traditionally has been viewed as the antithesis of the feminine woman.

> Female role models which incorporate the attributes of independence, objectivity, and assertiveness and thereby violate society's common image of femininity repel many men and women. Helen Hacker's study of working women

documents the ambivalence and disapproval facing the woman who displays "male" virtues: "Negative feeling may attach to her for being ambitious for herself directly or in furthering her own interests to the detriment of her family."

Hence, because of the normative expectations of marriage, the woman who has a taste for market work may, for that reason, choose not to marry or not to stay married.

Table 4.20 depicts a strong inverse relationship between marital commitment and the labor force attachment of mature women. The marital status categories are arranged in descending order of marital commitment, with never having been married representing the least commitment and being married with spouse present representing the greatest commitment. With one exception (married-spouse absent), there is a steady and steep increase in the average labor force attachment of women as marital commitment decreases. The finding regarding those married with spouse absent is difficult to interpret as spouses may be absent for a variety of reasons including service in the armed forces. In any case, those who have a taste for marriage (although not necessarily those who have a taste for their spouses) are significantly under-represented in the higher attachment categories.

There is continuing evidence of an incompatibility between marriage and labor force attachment for women. In keeping with the expectations described above that "unmarriage" reflects a taste for market activity, there are significant and positive associations between low marital commitment and educational attainment, favorable attitudes toward women's extra-familial labors, and motivation for work other than economic necessity. In contrast to previous conclusions regarding males, there is nothing in these findings to suggest that marital status can be interpreted "as a proxy for elements of personality and for physical and mental health defects which lower a man's prospective earnings and thus discourage labor force participation" as these elements would inhibit a stable marriage (Bowen and Finegan, 1969:44). Never-married women have greater educational attainment than married women and there are no important differences in health between those married (86 percent report their health as excellent or good) and those never-married (85 percent report excellent or good health).

TABLE 4.20: WOMEN'S LABOR FORCE ATTACHMENT BY MARITAL COMMITMENT (PERCENT BY COLUMN)

Type of Labor Force Attachment	Marital Status in 1967						
	Married Spouse Present	Married Spouse Absent	Widowed	Separated	Divorced	Never Married	
Career	10.0	2.6	16.5	22.8	30.5	61.7	
Strong	14.6	18.4	20.3	26.1	25.7	14.1	
Moderate	19.5	23.7	25.4	19.6	21.9	6.6	
Sporadic	22.8	14.5	21.2	14.0	10.7	4.3	
Casual	24.0	23.7	11.4	11.3	9.7	6.3	
None	9.0	17.1	5.1	6.2	1.6	7.0	
% of Total	84.5	0.7	2.1	3.3	4.4	5.0	
Mean LFA	37	35	48	54	60	71	

Given previous findings of negative association between enabling conditions (education and health) and age at first marriage, there are reasons to expect an inverse relation between age at first marriage for women and their labor force attachment in addition to the notion that early marriage reflects a taste for domesticity. As shown in Table 4.21 age at first marriage is not as strongly related to labor force attachment as marital status in 1967.

In keeping with expectation, women who married very young (under 16 years of age) are more likely than other ever-married women to have no labor force attachment. Women who marry late (age 25 or over) are more likely than other ever-married women to be found in the career category. However, these women are also more likely to have sporadic labor force attachment. Overall, age at first marriage appears to affect the labor force attachment of women only for the extremes: very young marriage or early marital commitment depresses participation slightly, while late marriage has a slight positive effect; no marriage is again the most positive influence on participation.

Of those who have ever been married, there is also some evidence that high work commitment generates "marital mobility." At least there is a significant association between having been married more than once and greater than average labor force attachment. The findings reported in Table 4.22 suggest that ever-married women who have been married more than once average five percent greater labor force attachment than women married only once. The difference in the moderate attachment category could well be expected on the basis of need during the period of unmarriage. However, the need for income does not explain the difference at the career level.

To summarize the findings about marital commitment, career women are more likely than other women to have low marital commitment: to be unmarried in 1967; or if married in 1967 to have married late; or if ever-married to have been married more than once. As reported below, those married respondents with high work commitment are also more likely than other married women to perceive their spouse as having liberal attitudes toward the wife's extra-familial work commitment.

Women with high work commitment who also had high marital commitment in 1967, were more likely to be

TABLE 4.21: WOMEN'S LABOR FORCE ATTACHMENT BY MARITAL COMMITMENT (PERCENT BY COLUMN)

Type of Labor Force Attachment	Age at First Marriage for Ever-Married in 1967						Total (of ever-married)
	age 15 or less	16-17	18-19	20-21	22-24	age 25 or greater	
Career	8.3	9.6	9.7	12.7	11.9	18.2	11.5
Strong	17.7	17.4	16.1	14.2	16.9	12.8	15.8
Moderate	21.9	23.3	21.3	18.3	17.3	16.5	19.8
Sporadic	22.5	17.8	21.8	21.2	21.5	28.7	21.8
Casual	14.9	20.5	25.3	26.1	23.5	15.3	22.5
None	14.8	11.4	5.8	7.4	8.9	8.5	8.5
Col Total	6.4	16.8	26.5	21.6	17.6	11.1	
Mean LFA	38	39	39	39	39	43	

TABLE 4.22: WOMEN'S LABOR FORCE ATTACHMENT BY MARITAL COMMITMENT
(PERCENT BY COLUMN)

Type of Labor Force Attachment	More Than One Marriage as of 1967 for Ever-Married		Total (of ever-married)
	No	Yes	
Career	11.1	14.5	11.5
Strong	15.5	17.2	15.7
Moderate	19.2	23.7	19.8
Sporadic	22.4	18.6	21.9
Casual	23.0	19.4	22.5
None	8.9	6.5	8.5
% of Total	86.7	13.3	
Mean LFA	38	44	

involved in "non traditional marriages," i.e., marriages in which the husband had favorable attitudes toward the wife's labor force activities. Table 4.23 reports that the large majority of husbands are either ambivalent or opposed to the wife's work for any reason. Only one-third of husbands are perceived as approving of the wife's employment. Such a finding supports the suggestion on page 107 that marriage affects a woman's taste for work directly by increasing the psychic costs of participation. At least this suggestion holds for two-thirds of mature married women. Moreover, those women for whom marriage does represent such a perceived cost, are significantly less likely to have strong labor force ties. The overwhelming majority of wives (88.6 percent) who perceive a strong orientation against their outside employment have sporadic, casual, or no attachment to the labor force.

Husband's attitude toward the wife's employment (as she perceives it) explains about 25 percent of the variation in married women's labor force attachment. Almost half (45.9 percent) of wives whose husbands strongly approve of their working are in the career and strong near-career categories contrasted to less than five percent (3.6 percent) of wives who report that their husbands are strongly opposed to their working outside the home. Being married to a non-traditional husband who is attitudinally supportive (or at least perceived as being supportive) of the wife's labor market activities is quite clearly a facilitating condition of labor force attachment, and the stronger the perceived support, the greater that attachment. Hence, the conclusion that when women with a taste for careers outside the home do marry, they tend to marry those who support their market activities.

Blau and Duncan report (1967:343) no substantial change in their models when characteristics of the wife are included. As they state: "the kind of marriage match a man makes does not loom large as a predictor of his occupational success." Our findings indicate that the kind of match a woman makes is quite important for her occupational endeavors. Indeed, the type of marriage is as important as the fact of marriage for women's labor force attachment.

Husband's attitude toward the wife working outside the home is a far more important facilitating condition than other characteristics of the husband, in particular his socioeconomic status. Similar to the

TABLE 4.23: WOMEN'S LABOR FORCE ATTACHMENT BY HUSBAND'S ATTITUDE IN 1967 (PERCENT BY COLUMN)

Type of Labor Force Attachment	Perceived Attitude of Husband Toward Wife Working Outside the Home					Total (of married)
	Like Very Much	Like Somewhat	Undecided	Dislike Somewhat	Dislike Very Much	
Career	22.5	14.5	12.5	6.1	0.8	10.2
Strong	23.4	22.6	19.0	12.2	2.8	14.7
Moderate	27.8	25.5	21.3	18.8	7.9	19.1
Sporadic	16.8	21.1	21.8	26.7	25.4	22.8
Casual	8.2	12.5	19.8	27.6	43.0	24.3
None	1.3	3.4	5.7	8.6	20.2	9.0
% of Total	16.5	17.7	19.8	19.5	26.5	
Mean LFA	56	49	43	33	18	37

findings for husband's income, there is a weak inverse relation (coefficient = -.05) between husband's educational attainment and wife's labor force attachment--accounted for primarily by the substantially higher representation of the wives of "college men" in the sporadic and casual categories. Overall, however, there is little difference in participation scores for wives of the least and most educated men (an average difference of less than four points). Nor are there marked differences in the labor force attachment of married women by the occupational classification of husbands (correlation ratio is .009).

Although the findings for husband's social class are less than deterministic of married women's labor force attachment, some of the findings are of interest in the light of previous studies. Bowen and Finegan (1969:155) hypothesized that the adjusted labor force participation rate of married women (obtained after controlling for other family income, schooling of the wife, color, age, presence of children, and employment status of the husband and all the other individual characteristics considered in their study) would be higher for the wives of professional-technical workers than for other wives. They based their hypothesis "on the grounds that men in professional-technical occupations might be relatively liberal in their attitudes toward working wives."

Bowen and Finegan (1969:155) concluded that "We could not have been more wrong." They found that "the wives of professional-technical workers had the lowest rate of any group of wives classified according to the occupation of the husband." Their adjusted participation rates are included in column 3 of Table 4.24. The adjusted participation rates for the wives of professional-technical workers is significantly lower than for the wives of service workers, clerical workers, operatives, and sales workers.

Rethinking the question of what relationship they should have expected to find, Bowen and Finegan (1969:156) suggest as one possibility "some correlation between the husband's educational attainment and his willingness to let his wife work." So, they suggest, the fact that the average educational attainment of male laborers is clearly the lowest of any nonfarm group may help to account for the low participation of their wives." Unfortunately, having no access to attitudinal data, Bowen and Finegan were unable to bring evidence to bear on their supposition. In this,

114

we are more fortunate.

The relationship between the adjusted participation rates of married women (taken from Bowen and Finegan) and the percent of husbands with liberal attitudes by husbands' occupational category is .64. As reported in Table 4.25 there is, moreover, the anticipated <u>inverse</u> relation between husbands' SES as indexed by average earnings and average education of men in these occupational categories and the percentage of husbands with liberal attitudes.

Noting a close relation (.91) between the adjusted participation rates and our average LFA scores by husbands' occupational groupings, the findings reported in Tables 4.24 and 4.25 show even higher rank-order correlations between the percent of husband with liberal attitudes and (1) average LFA and (2) percent of wives with LFA scores of 40 and above. Those coeffiients are .77 and .83 respectively. Agreeing with the findings of Bowen and Finegan, our findings indicate that women whose husbands have clerical, operative, and service jobs, average significantly greater labor force attachment than other married women; while women married to professional men average the least labor force attachment.

Whatever the facilitations in being married to a professional man, there appears to be little in the social milieu of such a marriage to facilitate labor force attachment. Perhaps, as Bowen and Finegan suggest (1969:155), the wives of such men feel that "their husband's occupation obligates them to participate in" community affairs and social activities. In other words, women married to professional men may have a greater investment in the role of wife and/or more demanding wife-role.

A negative association between the non-market activities of women and their labor force participation can be expected for several reasons. Briefly, an investment in children and other homemaking activities reflects a taste for and commitment to familial roles and, conversely, a distaste for market work and high opportunity costs for work outside the home. The findings are clearly consistent with this expectation.

As expected, there is a strong inverse relation between the number of children acquired by women and their labor force attachment.[2] Moreover, Table 4.26 depicts a linear relationship between labor force

TABLE 4.24: HUSBAND'S OCCUPATION BY LABOR FORCE PARTICIPATION OF WIVES, PERCENT WITH LIBERAL ATTITUDES, AVERAGE EARNINGS AND EDUCATION

Husband's Occupation	Average LFA of Wives Col. 1	% of Wives With LFA Scores > 40 Col. 2	Participation Rates (Bowen and Finegan) Col. 3	% of Husbands With Liberal Attitudes Col. 4	Average Earnings Col. 5	Average Years of School Col. 6
Clerical	42.2	50.2	38.9	35.2	8,536	12.5
Service	41.1	47.3	41.3	36.3	6,857	11.2
Operative	40.0	49.7	38.5	36.9	7,863	11.1
Manager	37.7	45.8	33.8	34.3	12,101	12.9
Sales	37.3	45.5	37.9	33.0	10,093	12.7
Craft	36.6	43.0	34.5	31.9	9,034	12.0
Labor	36.6	43.5	32.5	34.7	6,646	10.4
Professional	34.4	37.3	32.4	32.2	12,237	16.3

* Statistics taken from Bowen and Finegan (1969)

TABLE 4.25: RANK-ORDER CORRELATION COEFFICIENTS FOR VARIABLES IN TABLE 4.24

	(2) % LFA ≥ 40	(3) Part. Rates	(4) % Husband	(5) Earning	(6) Ed.
(1) Average LFA	.97	.91	.77	-.38	-.22
(2) % LFA ≥ 40		.81	.83	-.40	-.29
(3) Part. Rates			.64	-.45	-.33
(4) % Husbands				-.67	-.57
(5) Earnings					.95

attachment and number of children, suggesting that the crucial factor is not simply whether a woman has children but how many children she has.

The ages of children are also an important factor in labor force participation, although not so important as the simple quantitative aspect of child investment. Findings for this variable, presented in Table 4.27, reinforce the notion that a taste for children as expressed in a recent "acquisition" (the presence of a very young child in 1967) does depress labor force participation. With few exceptions (the presence of one older sibling 14-17), having a baby in the home is associated with less than average labor force attachment.

Much has been written about the complexities of the relationship between female labor force participation and fertility. The major question is whether a desire for children decreases the labor force participation of women or whether labor force participation decreases the desire for children. A complimentary and confounding question concerns the fecundity of women: Does an inability to have children increase labor force participation as a substitute endeavor? Fecundity (or the ability to bear children) is difficult to determine and changes for individuals through time. The findings reported here do mitigate the influence of differential fecundity to some extent as the child investment variables include children who have ever lived with respondents including those acquired through marriage and/or adoption. However, a rigorous attempt to untangle the confounding causal questions pertaining to differential fertility is beyond the intent of this study. The contention is only that women with many children and with young children can be perceived as expressing a taste for and investment in the traditional role of mother, and such domestic orientations do, as expected, depress labor market activity.

Of women who have acquired children, having children early in a woman's life is associated with significantly greater labor force attachment--an unexpected finding. Table 4.28 reports the participation patterns of women by the age at which they first acquired children. Women who first acquired children when less than 17 years of age are more likely than other women with children to have strong attachment to the labor force, whereas women who have children relatively late are concentrated in the

118

TABLE 4.26: WOMEN'S LABOR FORCE ATTACHMENT BY CHILD INVESTMENT (PERCENT BY COLUMN)

Type of Labor Force Attachment	Number of Children Acquired by 1967				
	None	1	2-3	4-5	6 or more
Career	54.2	22.7	9.4	5.7	5.5
Strong	17.8	19.2	16.6	13.1	11.8
Moderate	9.1	19.6	21.5	19.1	18.3
Sporadic	9.8	15.9	22.4	24.5	22.2
Casual	5.2	17.0	21.5	27.4	30.8
None	3.9	5.5	8.5	10.3	11.4
% of Total	10.2	9.9	46.3	22.5	11.1
Mean LFA	70	50	39	33	31

TABLE 4.27: WOMEN'S LABOR FORCE ATTACHMENT BY CHILD INVESTMENT (PERCENT BY COLUMN)

Age Distribution of Children Under Age 18 Acquired by 1967

Type of Labor Force Attachment	0-2	0-2 3-5	0-2 6-13	0-2 14-17	0-2 3-5 6-13	0-2 3-5 14-17	0-2 3-5 6-13 14-17	0-2 6-13 14-17	3-5	3-5 6-13	3-5 14-17	3-5 6-13 14-17	6-13	6-13 14-17	14-17	none under 18
Career	5.2	4.2	7.7	0.0	2.6	12.5	4.6	2.8	10.6	7.2	6.7	6.3	12.0	7.2	17.2	39.3
Strong	7.2	18.6	7.0	15.2	6.6	37.5	13.5	13.7	11.6	9.7	9.6	10.4	17.8	17.3	20.9	20.2
Moderate	24.7	14.4	16.0	48.5	14.3	6.3	11.8	14.1	18.1	15.1	19.2	21.6	20.5	25.0	23.1	14.3
Sporadic	28.4	32.6	29.0	12.1	29.6	18.8	22.4	17.3	25.1	29.6	16.3	21.4	21.0	21.6	13.7	11.9
Casual	12.4	17.7	30.8	12.1	35.1	25.0	35.0	38.7	16.1	30.5	29.8	32.2	21.1	21.0	16.6	9.3
None	22.2	12.6	9.5	12.1	11.8	0.0	12.7	13.3	18.6	7.8	18.3	8.0	7.5	7.9	8.5	5.0
% of Total	1.7	1.9	4.1	0.3	4.8	0.1	2.1	2.2	1.8	11.5	0.9	4.8	18.2	19.5	8.9	17.1
Mean LFA	31	34	31	38	25	46	28	28	36	32	29	32	41	39	47	61

sporadic category. The presence of a "built-in" babysitter is one obvious explanation for this unexpected finding. A more subtle possibility is that of early dissatisfaction with the requirements of the traditional homemaker-mother role.

The necessity of child care arrangements for employed women with children under the age of 18 is not related to the labor force behavior of women in the manner expected. Table 4.29 indicates that women who must make formal arrangements for substitute child care are significantly _more_ likely than other employed mothers to have strong labor force ties. Interpretation of this positive relation must be made with caution as the universe is restricted to employed women and, hence, selective recruitment is a consideratjon. However, once again, the suggestion is made that the crucial determinant for women's labor market activity is not simply the presence or absence of familial demands but, rather, women's tastes for their familial roles.

In regard to the suggested importance of women's tastes for the domestic sex-roles and the second explanation advanced for the unexpected relation between age at which women acquire children and their labor force attachment, there is a strong association between the age at which women acquire children and their attitudes toward child care. More specifically, women who had children early in life are significantly more likely than other married women to express negative attitudes toward child care activities in 1967. Perhaps informing such negative attitudes toward the mother role is the fact that women who begin their fertility behavior early (in particular, black women) are less likely to have the advantageous economic circumstances to facilitate the ideal mother role. Therefore, early realization of the responsibilities of motherhood may be responsible for subsequent labor market investment.

Before turning attention to the subjective sex-role investment of women as reflected in their attitudes toward women's roles, there are two more objective indicators of non-market tastes which are related to labor force participation. Tastes for a domestic life-style as expressed by investment in a home and housekeeping activities are more characteristic of women with low labor force attachment than of career women. In contrast to the findings of previous studies (Bowen and Finegan, 1969:107), which

TABLE 4.28: WOMEN'S LABOR FORCE ATTACHMENT BY CHILD INVESTMENT (PERCENT BY COLUMN)

Type of Labor Force Attachment	Age First Acquired Children					Total (of those with children)
	Less than 17	17 - 19	20 - 22	23 - 25	greater than 25	
Career	10.7	8.2	10.0	9.5	9.9	9.5
Strong	21.7	15.3	15.1	15.0	14.4	15.4
Moderate	20.4	23.7	19.5	18.7	18.4	20.2
Sporadic	25.4	19.3	20.7	20.8	29.7	22.2
Casual	13.0	22.3	27.3	27.8	18.0	23.7
None	8.8	11.1	7.4	8.2	9.5	9.0
% of Total	6.2	25.1	30.0	21.5	17.3	
Mean LFA	43	37	37	36	38	

122

TABLE 4.29: WOMEN'S LABOR FORCE ATTACHMENT BY CHILD INVESTMENT
(PERCENT BY COLUMN)

Type of Labor Force Attachment	Were Child Care Arrangements Necessary in 1967?		Total of employed with (children under 18)
	No	Yes	
Career	17.6	25.8	20.3
Strong	29.9	32.6	30.8
Moderate	33.9	28.6	32.2
Sporadic	15.7	10.3	13.9
Casual	2.9	2.8	2.9
None			
% of Total	67.6	32.4	
Mean LFA	58	63	60

123

showed no significant relationship between housing circumstances and women's labor force participation, the findings reported in Table 4.30 delineate a significant difference between the labor force patterns of women by whether they own or rent their dwellings. Rented dwellings are, on the average, smaller, require less investment of time and energy, and allow greater freedom to move than a home. In other words, rented dwellings require and so may reflect less commitment to homemaking.

As reported in Table 4.31, there are significant differences in the labor force attachment of married women by commitment to family and housekeeping activities in 1967. Bearing in mind that questions pertaining to such non-market activities were asked only of married respondents (and hence do not include those likely to be least committed to such activities-- namely, unmarried women), almost two-thirds of married respondents with no significant labor force attachment report family and housekeeping activities in addition to that considered "work." Approximately 60 percent of casual and sporadic workers report such domestic activities contrasted to only 50 percent of married career women.

Interestingly, married women with strong labor force ties were somewhat more likely than other married women to engage in entertainment, sports, and social activities away from home, while there were no significant differences in the labor force attachment of married women by whether they (a) engaged in other activities at home and (b) engaged in clubs, educational, or church activities. Again, the findings suggest that women's commitment to traditional female sex-role behavior of homemaker, wife and mother is the most important determinant of their labor force behavior.

In regard to subjective sex-role investment or women's expressed attitudes toward women's roles, two sets of attitudes were investigated. The first pertains to the traditional work of women, i.e., child- care and housekeeping activities. The second pertains to women's work outside the home. Unfortunately, questions concerning attitudes toward child-care and housekeeping were asked only of married respondents. Women with the greatest distaste for traditional female sex roles are likely to be unmarried and, therefore, not to be counted in the first set of findings pertaining to subjective sex-role commitment. However,

124

TABLE 4.30: WOMEN'S LABOR FORCE ATTACHMENT BY HOMEMAKING
            ACTIVITY (PERCENT BY COLUMN)

Type of Labor Force Attachment	Tenure in 1967		
	Owned	Rented	No Cash Rent
Career	12.0	19.7	12.3
Strong	15.3	15.8	22.9
Moderate	19.4	19.2	13.6
Sporadic	22.2	18.0	19.3
Casual	22.1	20.4	21.5
None	8.9	6.9	10.4
% of Total	71.5	25.2	3.3
Mean LFA	39	45	41

TABLE 4.31: WOMEN'S LABOR FORCE ATTACHMENT BY HOMEMAKING ACTIVITY
(PERCENT BY COLUMN)

Type of Labor Force Attachment	NonMarket Activity: Family or House Keeping Related Activities in 1967?		Total (of Married)
	Yes	No	
Career	8.8	11.7	10.0
Strong	13.7	15.8	14.6
Moderate	19.3	19.9	19.5
Sporadic	23.2	22.3	22.8
Casual	25.2	22.3	24.0
None	9.7	8.0	9.0
% of Total	57.2	42.8	
Mean LFA	36	40	37

even among women with high marital commitment (those married with spouse present in 1967), the expectation is that commitment to other dimensions of sex-role behavior will vary, and that such variation will be associated with variation in labor market behavior.

In keeping with the notion of selective recruitment, i.e., that women with a pronounced distaste for traditional sex-role behavior are likely to be unmarried, married women are in general quite positive toward traditional women's work of child care and housekeeping. Ninety-five percent report that they like caring for children and eighty-six percent enjoy housekeeping activities. The findings also lend partial support to the expectation that women with high marital commitment, who also have strong orientations toward other domestic sex-roles, will evidence less labor force attachment than other married women.

The findings reported in Table 4.32 strongly support the expectation that married women with positive attitudes toward the domestic sex-role of mother will have less commitment to the labor force. We have already noted that unmarried women (those with low marital commitment) average significantly greater labor force attachment than women with high commitment to the wife role, and among married women those with ambivalence or dislike for the traditional role of mother are more likely than other married women to be career or near-career participants in the American labor force.

The findings about attitudes toward housekeeping are less clear-cut. Group differences in average LFA are significant and in the same direction as observed for group differences in attitudes toward child care. However, those differences are much less pronounced (ranging from 37 for those who like housekeeping very much and those who like it somewhat to 45, 39, and 43 for those undecided, those who dislike it somewhat, and those who dislike it very much), and the overall association (chi-square) between categories of labor force attachment and housekeeping attitudes is not significant (at .01).

Table 4.33 records the summary findings for all respondents' attitudes toward women working outside the home. There is as expected a pronounced association between a liberal attitude toward women's places and strong labor force ties. These summary findings are comprised of responses to a series of three statements,

127

TABLE 4.32: WOMEN'S LABOR FORCE ATTACHMENT BY SEX ROLE COMMITMENT (PERCENT BY COLUMN)

Type of Labor Force Attachment	Attitude Toward Child Care in 1967						Total (of married)
	Like Very Much	Like Somewhat	Undecided	Dislike Somewhat	Dislike Very Much		
Career	9.0	10.1	29.2	20.6	23.0		10.0
Strong	14.5	13.8	25.8	15.4	26.2		14.7
Moderate	20.1	19.1	16.7	10.5	15.1		19.5
Sporadic	23.3	22.1	18.3	20.6	12.7		22.8
Casual	23.8	25.9	5.0	25.9	18.3		24.0
None	9.2	9.0	5.0	6.9	4.8		9.0
% of Total	75.5	19.3	1.3	2.6	1.3		
Mean LFA	37	37	58	43	52		37

which reflect varying degrees of conflict with traditional notions of "woman's place." Respondents were asked to record their feelings as such would pertain to the situation of a married woman with children between the ages of six and twelve taking a full-time job outside the home. The statements are as follows:

(I)   If it is absolutely necessary to make ends meet;
(II)   If she wants to work and her husband agrees;
(III)   If she wants to work, even if her husband does not particularly like the idea.

In general, findings for the individual questions support previous interpretations (see Oppenheimer, 1970; Havens and Gibbs, 1975) that the labor force participation of married women is condoned when it does not conflict with familial norms and condemned when such participation is perceived as conflicting with traditional sex-role behavior. When female labor force participation is seen as supportive of the family as in the case of family economic need, over 90 percent of mature American women condone the participation and almost two-thirds (64 percent) say it is definitely all right for the wife to provide such "secondary" support. When participation is motivated by a desire on the part of wives and does not go against husbands' wishes, strong agreement declines to one-third, and strong opposition increases to 14 percent. However, the majority still sanction a wife's work under this condition. When work outside the home is motivated by a desire on the part of the wife which the husband does not condone (a "selfish" desire?), well over three-fourths of the women (83.3 percent) express opposition to the wife's labor force participation.

In this way the attitudes of women and men are obviously intermingled. The overwhelming majority of women do not agree with wives working outside the home when such conflicts with husbands' desires, and a large majority of husbands are perceived as ambivalent or negative about women's work outside the home. This may provide a partial explanation for the finding that women with career orientations are likely to be unmarried--at least such unmarried status is one resolution for conflicting expectations.

In summation, the greater the subjective commitment to traditional sex-roles, the less the labor force attachment of women. Women's attitudes toward

TABLE 4.33: WOMEN'S LABOR FORCE ATTACHMENT BY ATTITUDE TOWARD WOMAN'S PLACE (PERCENT BY COLUMN)

Type of Labor Force Attachment	Summary of Attitudes Toward Women Working Outside The Home		
	Opposed (Conservative)	Ambivalent (Middle-of-the-road)	In Favor (Liberal)
Career	13.9	12.2	19.2
Strong	7.9	14.4	21.8
Moderate	16.0	18.8	21.0
Sporadic	20.2	22.2	18.1
Casual	28.3	23.2	15.8
None	13.8	9.3	4.2
% of Total	8.6	66.8	24.6
Mean LFA	34	38	50

130

domestic sex-role behavior and the traditional place of women may or may not be causes of their labor market behavior. The causal questions are, as usual, complex. For example, it may be that women without strong sex-role commitments are simply more inclined "to drift" into a career pattern and then to rationalize their labor market investment. However, negative attitudes regarding the traditional expectations associated with the subordinate role of wife and the dependent mother role can be said to facilitate women's labor force attachment. Moreover, low subjective commitment to familial role behavior as expressed in 1967, and low marital and child investment as reflected in marital status and quantity of children in 1967, are associated with the kind of continuing participation which results in the assessment of strong and career participation in 1971. This temporal distinction does give weight to the contention that tastes for sex-role behavior influence subsequent labor market behavior.

Tastes for market activity reflected in attitudes toward the job in 1967 are also related to career participation in 1971. Women who stated that they liked their jobs very much are significantly more likely than other women employed in 1967 to be in the career category. The findings are reported in Table 4.34.

We have seen that tastes for market work and distastes for domestic sex-role behavior do facilitate strong ties to the labor force for mature American women. Attention now turns to a set of environmental circumstances, in particular, characteristics of the job and of the market which may condition women's tastes for employment as well as the probability of finding employment.

Work Patterns and Conditions of Demand: Job and Market Characteristics

Certainly, the economic rewards attached to a job are an important job characteristic. Such rewards are indicative not only of pay necessary to cover the costs of employment, i.e., of substituting services in the home for married women, paying for transportation, etc., but also of the nature of the work, i.e., the importance and relative esteem associated with the job. Economic rewards are an important characteristic of job prestige and worker esteem, and, hence of job

131

TABLE 4.34: WOMEN'S LABOR FORCE ATTACHMENT BY ATTITUDE TOWARD JOB
(PERCENT BY COLUMN)

Type of Labor Force Attachment	Attitude Toward Job in 1967					Total (of those employed)
	Like Very Much	Like Fairly Well	Dislike Somewhat	Dislike Very Much		
Career	31.7	23.7	22.7	22.1		28.9
Strong	28.7	30.4	27.0	35.1		29.3
Moderate	27.1	28.8	25.9	28.6		27.6
Sporadic	10.7	13.7	19.5	3.9		11.8
Casual	1.8	3.4	4.9	10.4		2.5
None						
% of Total	65.6	29.5	3.5	1.5		
Mean LFA	65	61	58	61		64

132

attractiveness for most if not for all workers. In this regard, we found no significant difference among employed women as to whether good wages or liking the work were more important. Such can be explained on the grounds that good wages and interesting work are interrelated. Dead-end, routine type jobs are more likely than interesting jobs to be poorly rewarded economically as well as in other ways. So the economic rewards attached to a job are considered to reflect intrinsic job characteristics and also to indicate the market demand for qualified personnel (on this issue, see Bowen and Finegan, 1969:159).

There are many reasons to expect a strong relation between job wages and labor force attachment. The most obvious is that women with continuous participation are more likely than others to command high wages (a supply characteristic). Less obvious, perhaps, but of equal or greater significance is the suggestion that high rewards are an indication of job importance, job interest, and job demand. Most of us have a need to feel our activities are important, and one indication of such importance as related to a job is the salary attached to it. In this sense, wages are a characteristic of the job itself and reflect on the status of the incumbent. High wages are suggestive of high job status. Finally, economic rewards indicate opportunity costs for women: high wages indicate high opportunity costs for a woman who does not work; low wages indicate low oportunity costs for not working. This can also be perceived as a condition of demand, for wages are not determined by the potential worker except insofar as that worker acquires requisite off-the-job training.

The findings reported in Table 4.35 are strong support for the expectation that high job rewards in 1967 will be related to high labor force attachment in 1971. The overall association between job wages in 1967 and labor force attachment as measured in 1971 is .67. Wages in 1967 explain 46 percent of the variation in the labor force attachment of all women and 13 percent of variation in the labor force attachment of women employed during the 1967 survey week. Moreover, of women with wages in 1967, there is a direct linear relationship between the economic rewards received from working and labor force commitment. The majority of women who were able to earn over $3.50 an hour in 1967 are career participants in the American occupational structure.

TABLE 4.35: WOMEN'S LABOR FORCE ATTACHMENT BY JOB REWARDS (PERCENT BY COLUMN)

Type of Labor Force Attachment	Rate of Pay Per Hour in 1967						Total (of those with pay)
	Less than $.50	$.50-$1.24	$1.25-$1.74	$1.75-$2.50	$2.51-$4.50	greater than $3.50	
Career	16.2	14.2	13.8	31.9	46.7	52.0	27.1
Strong	21.6	23.6	23.1	29.9	27.5	32.5	26.5
Moderate	18.9	34.2	36.2	26.8	19.6	5.7	28.4
Sporadic	31.1	20.8	20.0	9.5	5.2	8.5	13.8
Casual	12.2	7.2	6.9	1.9	1.0	1.2	4.1
None							
% of Total	1.4	12.5	31.9	32.9	16.6	4.7	
Mean LFA	48	52	53	65	73	75	61

Among working women, the less they earned in 1967, the more likely they are to be represented in the sporadic and casual categories. The thorny causal question here is: Do women work less because they earn less or do they earn less because they work less? The present findings provide some clues to this question. Pay in 1967 is more strongly related to strength of participation in 1971 than is the 1971 wage rate (.67 and .60 respectively). In other words, past wages appear more deterministic of present labor force attachment than present wages. Certainly, differences in the unemployed group without wages is partly responsible for the differential associations, but not the entire picture.

Tables 4.36 and 4.37 offer a portrait of the wage mobility of women from 1967 to 1971. The first two wage levels in Table 4.35 have been collapsed for these calculations and the wage category of 0 (without wages) has been included. Hence wage level I for Tables 4.36 and 4.37 includes wages under $1.25. Table 4.36 depicts the percentage of women each wage origin supplies to the various wage levels in 1971. The column totals indicate the percentage of women in various wage destinations and these totals can be used to assess the relative contribution of each wage origin. For example, wage level I supplies 31.4 percent to wage level II in 1971, which is 3.5 times its expected contribution given the size of wage level II in 1971. Table 4.37 shows what proportion of the women in each wage level in 1971 were recruited from the various wage origins in 1967. For example, every wage level in 1971 has recruited more than ten percent of its members from the group without wages in 1967.

Looking first at the situation of supply, Table 4.36 indicates that women with wages in 1967 tend to remain out of the labor force unless they can find wages of $1.75 and higher. Of the 30 percent of women without wages in 1967 who have wages in 1971, 21 percent have wages of at least $1.75 an hour. In addition, with one notable exception, the greater the wage level in 1967, the less likely women are to be out of the labor force in 1971 (i.e., without wages). Twenty-eight percent of women with wages under $1.25 an hour (wage level I) in 1967 are out of the labor force in 1971. In other words, more than one-quarter of the women with low wages in 1967 dropped out of the labor force by 1971. For wage level II, there is about 20 percent attrition. The attrition rate continues to decline by wage level to about ten percent of those in

TABLE 4.36: 1967-1971 WAGE MOBILITY: OUTFLOW PERCENTAGES
(SUPPLY)

1967 Wage Level	1971 Wage Level						Total
	0	I	II	III	IV	V	
0	70.3	2.7	6.6	12.0	5.6	2.7	100.00
I	28.2	16.0	31.4	19.9	3.3	1.2	100.00
II	19.6	1.3	19.8	46.9	10.2	2.1	100.00
III	14.6	1.7	2.3	25.8	42.3	13.2	100.00
IV	9.4	0.3	1.2	7.4	27.2	54.5	100.00
V	17.5	0.0	0.0	2.4	6.9	73.2	100.00
Total	45.6	3.0	9.0	19.3	13.5	9.7	

TABLE 4.37: 1967-1971 WAGE MOBILITY: INFLOW PERCENTAGES (RECRUITMENT)

1967 Wage Level	1971 Wage Level						Total
	0	I	II	III	IV	V	
0	82.2	48.8	39.3	33.2	22.2	14.7	53.2
I	4.0	<u>34.9</u>	22.7	6.7	1.6	0.8	6.5
II	6.4	6.6	<u>33.0</u>	36.3	11.3	3.2	14.9
III	4.9	8.7	4.0	<u>20.6</u>	48.1	21.0	15.4
IV	1.6	0.9	1.0	3.0	<u>15.6</u>	43.7	7.8
V	0.8	0.0	0.0	0.3	1.1	16.6	2.2
Total	100.0	100.0	100.0	100.0	100.0	100.0	

wage level IV. The exception to this trend is the 17.5 percent attrition of women in the highest wage level, which is proportionately about as great an attrition rate as for wage level II.

Table 4.37 suggests a possible explanation for these attrition rates. Of women with wages in 1967, the greater their mobility from their wage origins, the less their attrition. Or, one could state, the greater the wage opportunities, the less the attrition. Looking at the major diagonal in Table 4.37, wage level I recruits about 35 percent of its members from wage level I. The comparable figures are 33 percent for wage level II, 21 percent for wage level III and 16 percent for wage level IV. Although not presented in tabular form, women in the wage level of $3.51 to $5.00 (within wage level V) in 1967 are less likely than women in wage level III to move upward in salary. Such suggests that wage discrimination in the form of blocked advancement may be responsible for the higher attrition of this group of women.[3]

Table 4.38 presents the findings for women's labor force attachment by the percentage of women working in the respondent's industry. Since sex-typed female jobs are, in general, less rewarding (see McNulty, 1967; and Stevenson, 1975), one would expect to find that such sex-typing is a depressant to labor market attachment for women. The relationship is in the direction expected. Women in industries which are more than 50 percent female in composition average somewhat less labor force attachment than women in industries less than 50 percent female. Yet most of the differences are not sizable and the exception, for women in those industries which are less than 10 percent female, is opposite to that expected.

The majority of working women in 1969 were in industries over 50 percent female in composition, although these women are not proportionately represented in the career category. Career women are disproportionately located among those women in industries (a) 10 to less than 20 percent female and (b) 35 but less than 50 percent female in composition. However, women in industries which were more than 90 percent male in 1969 are less likely than all other working women to have career ties to the labor force. Indeed these women are more likely to be characterized by sporadic and casual labor market activity. This is not altogether a surprising finding given the literature on sex discrimination, which indicates that

TABLE 4.38: WOMEN'S LABOR FORCE ATTACHMENT BY PERCENT OF WOMEN IN INDUSTRY, 1969
(PERCENT BY COLUMN)

Type of Labor Force Attachment	Industry Composition: Percent Female							Total of working women
	0.1-9.9	10.0-19.9	20.0-34.9	35.0-49.9	50.0-59.9	60.0-69.9	70.0-96.6	
Career	18.3	31.0	23.4	29.4	24.3	18.9	23.5	23.4
Strong	23.9	23.0	27.0	23.1	22.9	27.2	24.3	25.0
Moderate	20.0	29.2	30.5	26.2	29.3	26.4	26.3	27.4
Sporadic	25.2	13.8	14.6	15.3	19.0	20.5	17.4	17.9
Casual	12.7	3.0	4.0	6.0	4.2	6.8	8.3	6.1
None	0.0	0.0	0.5	0.0	0.3	0.2	0.2	0.2
% of Total	7.3	9.4	18.7	9.4	16.7	23.0	15.5	
Mean LFA	52	62	59	61	58	56	57	58

women attempting to enter predominantly male occupations are likely to encounter ubiquitous prejudice from employers, co-workers, and customers, as well as forms of "societal discriminations" (see Johnson and Staffors, 1975:210-211; and Madden, 1975:164).

In other words, problems of labor demand rather than of supply tend to depress the labor force participation of women in predominantly male occupations.[4]   At the upper ranges of female typecasting, demand problems associated with overcrowding may be operative (see Stevenson, 1975). These two interrelated problems of demand might be responsible for the observations that women in sex-typed industries, which are over 50 percent female in composition, are less represented in the higher ranks of labor force attachment (60 and above) than are women in jobs which are less than 50 percent but over 10 percent female.

The direct exploration of labor force size, reported in Table 4.39, supports the previous conclusion that size of place is not a uniform condition of women's labor force participation. Rather, both small and very large labor markets appear to depress labor force attachment. Women situated in 1967 in labor markets of 100,000 to 2,500,000 average somewhat higher labor force attachment than other women, while career women are disproportionately drawn from large labor markets of one million to two and one-half million. Overall, size of the labor force explains little of the variation in women's labor force attachment (less than one percent).

Of course, size of the labor force does not give an adequate picture of demand for particular labor resources--specifically women. The inadequacy of general areal pictures may also explain why no significant relation was found between area unemployment rates in 1967 and women's labor force attachment. A more relevant consideration for women is that of the demand for female labor in particular.

Using a measure of area demand for female labor devised by Bowen and Finegan (1969:174-175, 772-776), there is a strong association between environmental conditions and women's labor force behavior. Table 4.40 reports the findings for 1967 and 1971. The direction of the relationship is direct and linear for both time periods, but somewhat stronger in 1971 (the

TABLE 4.39: WOMEN'S LABOR FORCE ATTACHMENT BY SIZE OF AREA LABOR FORCE, 1967 (IN THOUSANDS) (PERCENT BY COLUMN)

Type of Labor Force Attachment	Less than 25	25-99	100-249	250-499	500-999	1000-2500	Greater than 2500
Career	10.5	12.8	15.7	17.3	15.2	21.5	12.7
Strong	15.5	15.0	19.5	16.0	16.9	11.2	12.8
Moderate	21.8	19.7	17.5	18.2	17.3	14.6	19.8
Sporadic	22.2	20.5	19.3	23.5	19.4	21.0	20.1
Casual	20.4	23.0	21.0	18.9	23.0	23.3	24.4
None	9.6	8.9	7.0	6.1	8.2	8.3	10.1
% of Total	21.8	24.1	16.2	12.9	7.7	5.6	11.7
Mean LFA	39	40	43	44	42	42	38

correlation coefficient is .10). In 1971, women in high demand areas averaged almost ten percent greater labor force attachment than women living in low demand areas. Hence an environment characterized by high demand for female labor does appear to have a positive impact on women's labor force attachment. Career participants are and have been located in areas of high demand, while those with no significant labor force attachment are located in areas of low demand. This finding appears to conflict with the findings regarding sex-typing. A possible resolution is that high demand is associated with an environment in which there are more positive sanctions for women workers in general. In this regard, women living in high demand areas have more liberal attitudes toward women's work outside the home.

General market conditions appear to exert little influence on the labor force attachment of women. Neither size of the labor market nor areal unemployment rates explain as much as one percent of the variation in women's labor force attachment. However, market conditions as they pertain to a broad endorsement of female labor force participation, specifically the areal demand for female labor, are associated with women's labor market behavior. Such area circumstances do have some importance, but by far the most important demand factors considered so far are those reflecting particular job characteristics.

Bowen and Finegan have stated (1969:127) that "the pecuniary and nonpecuniary rewards to work vary dramatically among occupations." Hence their question: Is the participation of women related to the occupation in which their most recent work experience took place? Using the non major non-farm occupational groupings, their finding (1969:128) "leaves no doubt concerning the statistical power of occupational group as a determinant of the wive's current labor force status."

The findings reported in Table 4.41 also leave no doubt as to the importance of occupational group for women's labor force attachment. Overall, occupation of respondents' most recent job explains three percent of the variation in their labor force attachment. There are, moreover, marked differentials in labor force attachment among occupational groupings, ranging from 56 for those in craft jobs to 33 for women in sales positions. About one-quarter of women employed in managerial, professional and craft occupations are career participants in the American labor force;

TABLE 4.40: WOMEN'S LABOR FORCE ATTACHMENT BY DEMAND FOR FEMALE LABOR, 1967 AND 1971 (PERCENT BY COLUMN)

Type of Labor Force Attachment	20-29		30-34		35-41	
	1967	1971	1967	1971	1967	1971
Career	11.9	11.6	13.2	13.8	18.4	19.6
Strong	14.7	14.9	15.9	15.7	16.1	18.3
Moderate	18.1	17.6	19.8	19.9	18.8	19.8
Sporadic	22.0	22.2	20.7	20.4	20.6	19.3
Casual	23.0	23.4	22.5	22.3	18.5	17.1
None	10.3	10.3	7.9	7.9	7.7	6.0
% of Total	24.5	25.4	53.3	56.3	22.1	18.3
Mean LFA	38	38	40	41	44	47

whereas the majority of women employed in sales, operative, private household, other service, non-farm labor, farm, and farm labor are characterized by sporadic and casual labor force participation.

In an attempt to explain the occupational differences in women's participation rates, Bowen and Finegan (1969:129) suggest that the higher a particular occupation ranks in earnings and psychic income, the greater the opportunity costs of withdrawing from the occupation and the higher the expected participation rate for women in that trade. Their findings are reported in Table 4.42. The unadjusted participation rates are the labor force participation rates for married women 30 years of age and older "with an occupation."[5] The adjusted participation rates are adjusted for the effects of color, presence of children, schooling, other family income, age, and employment status of husband (see Bowen and Finegan, 1969:127-128). The occupational categories are ordered by these adjusted participation rates.

The expected positive association between participation and earning opportunities (indexed by the median earnings in 1959 of women who worked 50-52 weeks that year) is clearly evident (Bowen and Finegan, 1969:130). However, the relation is "far from perfect." The rank-order correlation coefficient between the adjusted participation rates and median earnings is .70; while the relation between the unadjusted participation rates and earnings is only .29. This relatively low correlation again suggests the necessity for assessing differential investment in the labor force per se. As a case in point, Bowen and Finegan explain the apparent anamoly of private household workers (1969:131-132):[6]

> Private household workers (domestics) provide another interesting case. Women in this trade received by far the lowest earnings in 1959 of any major group ($922 for full-year workers), yet their adjusted participation rate (59 percent) was about as high as that of clerical workers, whose full-year earnings ($3,546) were nearly four times as large.
>
> A large part of the explanation for the unexpectedly high participation of domestics may lie in the prevalence of part-time work

TABLE 4.41: WOMEN'S LABOR FORCE ATTACHMENT BY OCCUPATION OF CURRENT OR LAST JOB, 1971
(PERCENT BY COLUMN)

Type of Labor Force Attachment	Occupation of Current or Last Job, 1971											
	Prof.	Mgr.	Cler.	Sales	Craft	Oper	P.H.H.	Service	Farm	Farm Lab	Labor	Total
Career	23.4	25.5	16.3	6.2	24.1	13.1	6.5	9.0	3.2	5.8	8.9	14.6
Strong	20.4	23.1	14.6	11.5	25.0	18.5	15.1	14.0	6.5	15.8	6.7	16.2
Moderate	15.8	21.3	18.6	15.7	24.1	22.3	17.2	26.2	19.4	15.8	20.0	19.9
Sporadic	15.6	18.0	21.3	30.9	13.8	18.7	22.7	25.4	35.5	29.9	55.6	21.7
Casual	19.1	8.5	22.3	28.0	10.3	22.5	33.2	22.1	35.5	28.0	8.9	22.1
None	5.6	3.6	6.8	7.7	2.6	4.9	5.3	3.3	0.0	4.8	0.0	5.5
% of Total	12.2	4.6	36.1	6.3	1.1	16.4	4.4	15.1	0.3	2.9	0.4	
Mean LFA	49	55	42	33	56	43	34	40	29	35	39	42

TABLE 4.42: WOMEN'S OCCUPATIONAL GROUP, BY LABOR FORCE PARTICIPATION AND EARNINGS: FINDINGS REPORTED BY BOWEN AND FINEGAN

Occupational Group	Percent of Population	Labor Force Participation Rate Unadjusted	Labor Force Participation Rate Adjusted	Median Earnings in 1959 of Full-year Female Workers
Managers	3.8	73.6	70.0	$3,800
Professional Workers	11.0	64.4	67.3	4,186
Craftsmen	1.4	64.4	62.9	3,555
Clerical Workers	33.5	55.9	61.0	3,546
Private Household Workers	4.3	72.8	59.0	922
Other Service Workers	13.5	61.7	58.2	2,102
Operatives	20.8	59.8	57.3	2,911
Sales Workers	11.6	51.1	48.7	2,370
Laborers	0.4	53.9	47.6	2,863

* Taken from Bowen and Finegan (1969:Table 5-7, p. 128).

in this occupation, since work of this kind
is less of a hindrance to work at home.

Comparable findings from this research are
presented in Table 4.43. Although the median income
figures have the same rank order for the two studies,
the labor force scores do not. The relationship
between the adjusted participation rates of Bowen and
Finegan and our labor force attachment scores is .75
(the rank-order correlation coefficient by major
occupational group). Moreover, the relation between
these LFA scores and the median income of women in 1969
is .83--significantly higher than the relation observed
for Bowen and Finegan.

The major discrepancy observed in the present
relation between female labor force attachment and
earnings opportunities, lies in the higher than
expected participation of craftsmen and managers; both
of which average substantially higher labor force
attachment than female professional workers. Bowen and
Finegan (1969:130-131), noting the difference between
managers and professional workers, may have provided an
explanation for the higher labor force attachment of
managers and craftsmen.

Differences in earnings clearly cannot
be the explanation, however, for the higher
adjusted participation rate of managerial
workers (70 percent) than of professional
workers (67 percent), since the women who
were classified as professional workers
earned almost $400 more in 1959 (on the
average) than the women in the managerial
occupations. Nor does it seem plausible to
attribute this participation differential to
differences in the psychic income received by
professional workers and managers--if
anything, the differential in psychic income
as in money income should favor the
professional group.

In our judgment, the main explanation
for the difference in adjusted participation
rates between the mangerial and professional
groups lies in the differing characteristics
of the two occupational groups with regard to
ease of re-entry. The educational and
acquired skills of the professional worker
are likely to be rather "general" in that
they can be put to the service of any number

TABLE 4.43: WOMEN'S OCCUPATIONAL GROUP BY LABOR FORCE ATTACHMENT
AND EARNINGS: FINDINGS FROM PRESENT RESEARCH

Occupational Group	Percent of Population	Mean LFA	Median Earnings in 1969 of Full-Year Female Workers
Craft	1.1	56	$5,370
Managers	4.6	55	6,246
Professional	12.2	49	7,172
Operatives	16.4	43	4,432
Clerical	36.1	42	5,366
Service	15.1	40	3,666
Labor	0.4	39	4,170
Private Household	4.4	34	1,792
Sales	6.3	33	3,809

of potential employers. Not even the vagaries of state licensing laws, for example, prevent school teachers from transferring their skills from one state to another; and within a single state (or community), movement into and out of the labor force is quite feasible for teachers, as well as for other professional workers. The knowledge and skills of managers, on the other hand, are likley to be much more "specific," to the particular firms in which they have gained their experience. Consequently, a managerial "drop-out" is likely to have a much more difficult time re-entering the labor market at more or less the same level of pay and responsibility that she enjoyed in her former job. Thus, women who have attained managerial positions may be especially reluctant to withdraw from the labor force, given the substantial opportunity costs involved.

Certainly, the same argument regarding "specific" skills can be made for the craft worker as for the managerial worker. In addition, the loss of seniority within a particular industry (whether unionized or not) might be even more detrimental for the craftsman who is a woman than for a managerial worker.

In any event, the findings of this and previous studies, do suggest that elements of occupational status are strongly related to women's labor force attachment. Indeed the strongest relationship discovered in this research is that between previous job rewards and women's labor force attachment.

Notes
Chapter Four

[1]These terms are borrowed from Sobol (1963:Chapter 3) although the interpretation of these terms and the variables used as indicators are not the same.

[2]This variable includes all children, natural and otherwise, who ever lived with the respondent. Hence, these findings more nearly express the desire for children as a woman who is not able to give birth can acquire children in other ways.

[3]Women in relatively high status positions may also experience greater frustration from their lack of mobility having higher expectations and higher investment in their jobs. In this regard, 50 percent of women in wage level V in 1967 had completed 16 or more years of school.

[4]Further research is needed to explore the effects of sex-typing per se on the job satisfaction and tenure of workers. For example, an important question pertains to the structurally generated conditions which may inhibit efforts to move women into male dominated occupations. It is possible that efforts to move a few women into such occupations are likely to meet with little success because of an environment which is hostile to or unsupportive of their presences.

[5]This means a woman who was either in the experienced civilian labor force during the census week or who was not in the ECLF but who had done some market work during the preceding decade.

[6]Remember that their adjusted rates control for the effects of large numbers of black women and women with low other family income working in this occupational group.

CHAPTER FIVE

SUMMATION AND CONCLUSIONS

The present study suggests that approximately one in every six mature women in the United States is a career participant in the labor force. Phrased another way, of all mature women with work experience, 15 percent have worked full time, year around, and continuously since leaving school. This figure is undoubtedly lower than the figure for men at the present time, but it is far greater than either popular or expert opinions have previously suggested. In addition, there is every reason to expect an increase in the career participation of women as younger women respond to better career opportunities, and as women are more likely to be characterized by circumstances significantly related to career investments in the American labor force. These circumstances of mature women, most likely to be reflected in a career type of labor force participation, are summarized below.

Before beginning this summary description of mature career women, it is important to recognize that summaries concentrate on aspects of similarity (or aspects of central tendency) rather than on aspects of differences. Hence, the summary should not be interpreted as indicating that all career women have the same characteristics. Indeed, such an interpretation would only serve to support the kind of statistical discrimination that already is used to the disadvantage of women in the labor force and to the disadvantage of a society which can ill afford to waste valuable human resources either through ignorance of the facts or misinterpretation of the facts.

General Characteristics of Career Women

Women who are, at present, career participants in the labor force are more likely than other women of the same age to have experienced the following recruitment circumstances:

151

(1) To have a mother who worked outside the home;
(2) To have high human capital investment;
(3) To live in highly urbanized areas;
(4) To have liberal spouses or be unmarried;
(5) To have small families;
(6) To have a taste for market work with relatively low subjective commitment to traditional sex-roles;
(7) To have jobs which are economically rewarding.

As previously stressed, these circumstances are not shared by all career women, but they are more "typical" of career women than of other mature women. In addition, not all of the circumstances are of equal importance in the effort to summarize the influences on women's work stability.

With regard to the notion of discriminating the relative importance of influences on women's market behavior, the level of economic rewards attached to jobs (7) appears to be a very powerful influence on women's lifetime supply of labor. Although the job characteristic of wages is a very important influence, other important influences reflect tastes for market work, including a relational-attitudinal variable of husband's attitude toward the wife's employment (4). In summation, it does appear that demand conditions reflecting characteristics of the job and supply conditions reflecting, in particular, the "facilitating" tastes for market work are among the most important recruitment circumstances. Such propensities for market work can, however, be summarized more rigorously and exactly with the aid of simple multivariate models of labor force attachment. For those readers who are interested in a summary of other bivariate relations, as well as a comparison with findings for 1977, they are referred to the Appendix material (Table A.3).

A Summary (Explanatory) Model of
Influences on Work Stability

Having analyzed the individual effects of various social origin and recruitment variables on the labor force attachment of mature American women, we are now prepared to look at a simplified model of the major influences. Table 5.1 presents an explanatory model of women's labor force attachment based on five of the major correlates. This summary model indicates both the individual effects and the net impact of five variables on women's labor force attachment. This model summarizes the effects of race, health, marriage (both the fact and type), children, and previous earnings level on the labor force attachment scores of mature American women. More specifically, Table 5.1 indicates the gross impact of various conditions on women's average LFA scores expressed as unadjusted deviations from the grand mean and the net impact of these conditions expressed as adjusted deviations from the grand mean (adjusted for the influence of other variables in the model). This table also reports the unadjusted correlation coefficient and the adjusted (or partial) correlation coefficient for each variable in the model. Finally, the table reports the coefficient of determination (R^2), or the amount of variation in women's labor force attachment scores explained by the five variables in the model. The five variables in the model together explain 61 percent of the variation in the labor force attachment scores of mature American women. Hence, this model explains more of the individual-level variation in female labor market behavior than previous models based on labor force status.

With regard to the impact of specific variables in the model, the most important demand condition and the most important single determinant of labor force attachment is previous earnings level. However, conditions of marriage also exert a powerful influence on observed levels of labor force attachment. Looking first at the variable marital investment, no marital investment (being unmarried in 1967) provides the greatest impetus to women's labor force attachment followed closely by low marital investment (being married to a non-traditional spouse with liberal attitudes towards "women's place"). As depicted in Table 5.1, being involved in a traditional marriage decreases labor force attachment by an average of 23 points. However, when other variables are controlled, being involved in a liberal marriage appears more facilitating of women's labor force attachment than being unmarried! Acting alone, marital investment (including fact and type of marriage) explains 25 percent of the variation in the labor force attachment of mature women.

The quantitative aspects of child investment also explain a significant proportion of the total variation in women's labor force attachment. Having no children in 1967 increases labor force attachment by about 30 points, whereas high child investment decreases labor force attachment by about 10 points. However, the

TABLE 5.1: MAJOR DETERMINANTS OF LABOR FORCE ATTACHMENT FOR MATURE AMERICAN WOMEN

Variable	Category	Unadjusted Deviations	beta	Adjusted Deviations	beta
Race			.10		.05
	White	- 1.2		- .6	
	Black	8.5		3.7	
	Other	1.6		3.0	
Health			.15		.08
	Excellent	2.6		1.4	
	Good	.7		.2	
	Average	- 7.2		- 3.0	
	Poor	-18.3		-10.5	
Marriage[**]			.49		.20
	Unmarried	15.9		5.0	
	Married - very supportive	14.9		7.6	
	- moderately supp.	8.9		4.0	
	- ambivalent	2.1		.9	
	- moderat. unsupp.	- 7.5		- 3.0	
	- very unsupport.	-23.2		- 9.6	
Children			.36		.14
	none	28.0		11.2	
	one	9.4		3.7	
	two-three	- 1.9		- .8	
	four-five	- 7.5		- 2.9	
	six or more	-10.4		- 4.0	
Previous salary[***]			.74		.60
	≥ $10,000	21.4		14.6	
	7,000-9,999	38.0		28.3	
	5,000-6,999	36.8		29.4	
	3,000-4,999	29.1		24.4	
	1,500-2,999	20.1		16.9	
	500-1,499	8.8		6.9	
	500	-17.9		-14.6	
Grand Mean		40.6			
R^2					.610
(R)					(.781)

[*] Sample limited to those residentially stable 1967-1971 (about 6% missing)
[**] combined variable reflecting both the fact and type of marriage
[***] wage and salary income in 1966; all other variables measured in 1967.

impact of children is substantially reduced when conditions of health, marriage, attitudes, and salary are held constant. While having none or one child are still associated with increased levels of labor force attachment, having two children or more has only a slight depressing effect on women's labor force attachment.

Similar to the adjusted effects of children, respondent's attitudes toward women's place do not appear to have a marked effect on adjusted rates of labor force attachment. In other words, attributes of health, marriage, children, and salary explain most of the original (unadjusted) variations in labor force attachment observed for respondent's attitudes.

The most powerful variable in this model is that of previous earnings level. This variable is associated with substantial variation in labor force attachment scores and appears less influenced by other variables in the model. Of interest here is the observation that the largest increment in both unadjusted and adjusted labor force attachment scores is associated with the middle salary ranges. Hence it appears that good salaries (rather than the highest salaries) have the most positive impact on women's involvement in the labor force.

While conditions of health are significantly related to women's labor force attachment the most important influence is negative. Poor health is a powerful deterrent to labor force attachment, depressing attachment scores by 18 points from the grand mean. In other words, women who report poor health average labor force attachment scores less than the original sample of mature women. Even when other conditions related to marriage, children, attitudes, and previous salary level are controlled, poor health still depresses average labor attachment scores by ten points.

Conditions related to marriage (the fact and type of marriage) also exert marked positive and negative effects on women's labor force attachment. The average LFA scores for unmarried or women married to liberal spouses are substantially higher than the grand mean. On the other hand, a traditional marriage in which the husband disapproves of the wife's employment appears to have a decidedly negative impact on women's labor force attachment.

Investment in the traditional familial role of mother also appears to have a marked effect on labor force attachment. Unadjusted scores for women with no children average 28 points above the grand mean, while women with one child also have higher than average LFA scores. Not surprisingly, women with many children average substantially less attachment to the labor force.

Subjective sex-role investment in 1967 does not exert as much influence on women's labor market behavior as marital and child investment, and that influence appears largely explained by other variables in the model.

Finally, in regard to the original point about efforts to explain female labor force participation, the present effort to access differentials in women's labor market behavior has been rewarded by relatively high explanatory power. Sixty-one percent of individual level variation in labor force attachment is explained by the five correlates.

Differences Between Black and Nonblack Women

Given the observation of a sizable difference in the average labor force attachment scores of black and nonblack women, this section offers a brief investigation of this difference. As suggested earlier, the differential in labor force attachment scores between black and white women cannot be attributed to higher levels of part-time participation for black respondents. To the contrary, black women evidence higher levels on all dimensions of the labor force attachment index than white respondents.

	A/B	C	D	Mean LFA
White	.38	.20	.21	40
Black	.47	.26	.26	50
Other	.38	.25	.24	44

Although part-time employment does not explain the ten point differential, there are attributes of social origins and recruitment which appear (1) to decrease the observed differential between black and white women, (2) to increase the observed differential, and/or (3) to reverse the differential in favor of white women.

Average LFA scores for black and white women by selected social origin and recruitment characteristics are reported in Table 5.2. Observed differences in average labor force attachment are less between black and white women with the following characteristics:
differences decreased
poor health (1)
would work if unnecessary (0)
liberal attitudes (3)
like job very much (1)

On the other hand, differences in average labor force attachment scores increases between black and nonblack respondents with these characteristics:
differences increased
fathers education greater than 16 years (19)
respondent's education greater than 16 years (30)
excellent health (15)
two or three children (15)
residence in high demand area (15)

Finally, differences are reversed for black and nonblack women with the following characteristics:
differences reversed--average LFA for white women exceeds that for black women
liberal husband (-2)
no children (-5)
never married (-24)
For these circumstances, the labor force attachment of white women exceeds that for black women.

Differences in these influences on labor force attachment are summarized in the explanatory models in Tables 5.3 and 5.4. In general, explanatory power is higher for white women than for black women. Regarding the situation of supply, enabling conditions are more important for the labor force attachment of black women while facilitating conditions are more deterministic of the labor force attachment of white women. Regarding conditions of demand, job rewards in 1966 comprise the most important determinants for both groups of women although job rewards are less affected by the influence of other variables for black women. Additionally, as could be expected, general market conditions are more important to the labor market activities of black women than they are to white women.

The characteristics of black career women differ in many respects from those observed for white women (see Table 5.5). Most notably regarding social

157

TABLE 5.2: BLACK-WHITE DIFFERENTIALS IN LABOR FORCE ATTACHMENT

Variable	Attribute	Black	White	Dif (Δ)
		Average LFA Scores		
Social Origins				
at age 16				
	City ≥ 100,000	52.7	41.6	11.1
	farm or ranch	49.9	41.3	8.6
	Mother employed	50.7	42.1	8.6
	Father's education ≥ 16 yrs	55.2	35.8	19.4
	Mother's education ≥ 16 yrs	52.8	40.3	12.5
Recruitment: Supply				
Enabling conditions				
	Respondent's education ≥ 16 yrs	75.3	44.8	30.5
	Other training	57.8	45.3	12.5
	Excellent health	56.9	41.9	15.0
	Poor health	24.2	23.3	.9
Precipitating conditions				
Work Commitment				
	Would work if unnecessary	65.9	65.6	.3
	Other Household resources:			
	Husbands Income ≥ 7000	34.7	28.9	5.8
Facilitating conditions				
Marital Commitment				
	Married w/spouse present	47.6	36.3	11.3
	never-married	51.4	75.6	-24.2
	Husband's attitude: Liberal	54.2	55.9	- 1.7
	Conservative	24.3	17.4	6.9
Children				
	None	65.0	70.3	- 5.3
	2-3	52.9	37.7	15.2
Attitudes	Liberal	52.2	48.9	3.3
Characteristics of Market Place				
Current Residence				
	In Central City of SMSA	50.4	42.4	8.0
	Outside SMSA	48.2	38.3	9.9
	Length of Residence - 30 yrs.	48.9	40.8	8.1
	High for 1971	59.5	44.5	15.0
	1967	57.4	42.2	15.2
Characteristics of Job				
	Like job very much	66.3	64.9	1.4
	Salary - 7000 66	72.6	63.2	
	70	83.7	77.1	6.6
Occupational Group				
	Professional	68.3	47.4	20.9
	Managerial	66.6	55.1	11.5
	Clerical	58.7	41.3	17.4
	Sales	50.5	31.9	18.6
	Craft	73.4	54.7	18.7
	Operative	52.2	41.4	10.8
	Private Household	41.6	25.6	16.0
	Service	52.0	37.0	15.0
	Farm	45.4	23.8	21.6
	Farm labor	33.0	35.6	- 2.6
	labor	36.7	40.6	- 3.9

TABLE 5.3: MAJOR DETERMINANTS OF LABOR FORCE ATTACHMENT FOR MATURE WHITE WOMEN IN THE UNITED STATES

Variable	Category		Unadjusted LFA	Beta	Adjusted LFA	Beta
Marital investment in 1967				.52		.21
	None		59.2		44.8	
	Low:	1	55.8		47.4	
		2	48.4		43.7	
		3	41.1		40.4	
		4	31.7		36.8	
	High:	5	17.3		30.4	
Child investment in 1967				.39		.16
	None		79.4		51.7	
	Low:	1	47.9		43.3	
		2	37.5		38.4	
		3	31.4		36.3	
	High:	4	26.8		35.0	
Subjective sex-role investment in 1967				.18		.05
	Low:	1	48.6		41.5	
		2	37.3		39.1	
	High:	3	32.6		36.7	
Job rewards in 1966				.74		.60
	None		22.2		25.6	
	Low:	1	46.7		45.2	
		2	58.8		55.6	
		3	68.9		64.0	
		4	77.6		69.3	
		5	77.5		67.2	
	High:	6	63.2		56.6	

Grand Mean = 39.4 R^2 = .62
(N = 3246)

[1] Combined categories: none=unmarried; low=non-traditional marriage (husband strongly in favor of wife working); high=traditional marriage (husband strongly opposed to wife working).

[2] Wage and salary income in 1966.

TABLE 5.4: MAJOR DETERMINANTS OF LABOR FORCE ATTACHMENT FOR MATURE BLACK WOMEN IN THE UNITED STATES

Variable	Category		Unadjusted LFA	Beta	Adjusted LFA	Beta
Ability to work in 1967				.29		.11
	Low:	1	24.6		39.2	
		2	39.4		46.7	
		3	51.3		49.7	
	High:	4	56.9		52.3	
Marital investment in 1967				.27		.13
	None		51.8		50.8	
	Low:	1	54.3		53.1	
		2	52.6		49.2	
		3	50.4		48.3	
		4	47.1		47.7	
	High:	5	24.0		38.4	
Child investment in 1967				.30		.11
	None		65.1		57.3	
	Low:	1	60.5		53.0	
		2	52.5		47.9	
		3	45.0		46.9	
	High:	4	39.4		48.1	
Job rewards in 1966				.70		.62
	None		27.1		29.4	
	Low:	1	56.8		56.4	
		2	68.1		66.3	
		3	71.0		68.1	
		4	78.2		75.2	
		5	82.8		77.6	
	High:	6	72.6		70.2	

Grand Mean = 49.3 R^2 = .52
(N = 1236)

[1] Health: low= poor; high = excellent

[2] Combined categories: non=unmarried; low=non-traditional marriage (husband strongly in favor of wife working); high= traditional marriage (husband strongly opposed to wife working).

[3] Wage and salary income in 1966.

160

origins, black career women are twice as likely to come from farm origins and families in which the mother was employed. Regarding enabling conditions, black women are less likely to report excellent health.

With regard to precipitation conditions, black women are more likely to report that they would work even if unnecessary and less likely to have husbands with high incomes. For facilitating conditions, mature black women are less likely to be married with spouse present and also less likely to be never-married. Of those who are ever-married, black women are more likely to have children.

Black women are more likely to be living in metropolitan centers and in areas characterized by a high demand for female labor. They are less likely to like their work or to receive high salaries. Finally there are marked differentials in the occupational destinations of black and nonblack women. Most notably, career black women are eight times more likely than white women to attain service positions and only half as likely to have white-collar destinations.

Such observations of difference between the circumstances of white and of black career women underscore, once again, the dangers of generalizing about or "typifying" women. There is considerable variability in recruitment circumstances among career women as there is tremendous diversity in the work patterns of mature women.

Having now identified different populations of working women on the basis of their involvement in the American occupational structure and explored differences in the background and recruitment characteristics of these women, we are prepared to begin with more rigorous analysis of women's attainments in the American occupational structure.

TABLE 5.5: SELECTED CHARACTERISTICS OF MATURE CAREER WOMEN BY RACE:
PERCENTAGE OF CAREER WOMEN FOR EACH CHARACTERISTIC

	White	Black
Social Origins		
Residence at Age 16		
City ≥ 100,000	23.5	25.7
Farm or ranch	20.7	40.4
Mother Employed	34.8	63.8
Father's education ≥ 16 yrs	5.5	2.3
Mother's education ≥ 16 yrs	4.4	2.7
Recruitment: Supply		
Enabling Conditions:		
Respondent's education ≥ 16 yrs	13.4	14.3
Other Training	31.5	34.3
Excellent Health	52.9	41.9
Precipitating Conditions:		
Work commitment: Would work if unnecessary	67.1	73.5
Other Household Resources: Husband's		
Income - 7,000*	14.6	0.0
Facilitating conditions:		
Marital Commitment		
Married with spouse present	61.0	53.1
Never-married	24.2	13.1
Husband's attitude: liberal*	36.7	35.2
Children		
Has *	74.6	83.6
none		
2-3	31.2	28.6
Attitudes: Liberal	31.5	39.2
Characteristics of Market Place:		
Current Residence		
In central city of SMSA	32.6	62.7
Outside SMSA	31.7	27.0
Length of residence - 30 yrs	41.1	39.3
High demand for female labor	23.0	38.0
Characteristics of Job:		
like very much	73.6	62.2
salary ≥ 7,000	11.4	6.9
Occupational group		
White-collar	77.5	34.6
Blue-collar	15.7	23.6
Service	5.6	41.2
Farm	1.2	.4

* of those married

APPENDIX

The appendix contains a more complete and technical description of the LFA measure and its component dimensions. It also contains information pertaining to subsequent years of the NLS data set. Table A.3 indicates that there was little change in the correlates of labor force attachment between 1971 and 1977, due, in large part, to the longitudinal (i.e., cumulative) nature of the LFA measure.

TABLE A.1: DISTRIBUTIONS FOR COMPONENT DIMENSIONS OF LFA
THROUGH 1977 (% by row)*

| | Hours Per Week | | | |
	0	1 - 20	21 - 39	>40 or more
C67	45.6	9.1	12.9	32.5
C68	43.3	12.0	12.4	32.3
C69	47.2	8.7	13.3	30.8
C71	47.4	9.0	15.7	27.8
C72	45.4	9.6	14.2	31.9
C74	36.5	10.5	15.5	37.5
C76	38.0	10.5	16.2	35.2
C77	45.2	8.8	17.4	28.6

| | Weeks Per Year | | | |
	0	1 - 26	27 - 49	50 - 52
D67	41.8	14.5	14.2	29.5
D68	44.3	13.1	18.8	23.9
D69	39.5	11.6	17.4	31.4
D71	36.2	12.4	20.9	30.4
D72	38.5	9.3	21.9	30.4
D74	35.6	9.8	15.0	39.6
D76	37.3	9.4	13.9	39.3
D77	39.1	6.7	14.0	40.2

*N = 3945 using a base for 1977.

164

TABLE A.2: DISTRIBUTION OF CAREER PATTERNS 1971 – 1977*

	Career	Strong	Moderate	Sporadic	Casual	None
LFA 1971	14.5	17.5	19.0	20.3	21.0	7.7
LFA 1972	14.1	17.7	19.1	21.5	20.5	7.0
LFA 1974	14.4	17.9	19.3	22.5	20.0	5.9
LFA 1976	14.4	18.0	20.3	22.5	19.7	5.2
LFA 1977	14.2	17.8	20.7	22.5	20.0	4.8

*Based on 1977 N (3945) and using a general computing formula for LFA:
LFA – $[A/B + \Sigma C/6Yn + \Sigma D/6Yn]$ 50 where the denominator for ΣC and ΣD
is six (6) times the number of years used to compute the equation
(thus the denominator in 1971 is 24, whereas in 1974 it is 36, and in
1977 it is 48).

165

TABLE A.3: ILLUSTRATIVE COMPARISON OF INFLUENCES ON THE LABOR
FORCE ATTACHMENT OF MATURE WOMEN, 1971 (N = 4551)
AND 1977 (N = 3945)

	Correlation*	
Influence	1971	1977
Social Orgins		
(1) Race (VAR 0025)	.091	.105
(2) Mother's Ed. (VAR 0568)	n.s.	n.s.
(3) Father's Ed. (VAR 0565)	n.s.	n.s.
Enabling Conditions		
(4) Health VAR 0358)	.123	.159
**(5) Education (VAR 0838)	.085	.145
(6) Residence (VAR 0077)	.068	.046
Precipitating Conditions		
(7) Husband's Income		
(VAR 0452 + VAR 0453)	.063	.060
Facilitating Conditions		
(8) Age (VAR 0024)	n.s.	n.s.
(9) Marital Status (VAR 0026)	.296	.244
(10) Husband's Attitude		
(VAR 0338 + 0339)	.484	.446
(11) Respondent's Attitude		
(VAR 0336)	.146	.134
Market and Job Characteristics		
(12) Wages (VAR 0450 + VAR 0451)	.692	.613
***(13) Occupational Group		
(VAR 2086 + VAR 0764)	.098	.059

*Correlation from simple (one-way) analysis of variance with
F-test.

**Different recode procedures in 1971 and 1977 make this com-
parison unreliable.

***Different temporal locations for these variables make this
comparison unreliable.

166

TABLE A.4: PROPENSITIES FOR LABOR FORCE ATTACHMENT

Condition	Indicating Effects of	Association Expected	Association Direction	Observed Strng.**
I. SUPPLY	WORKER CHARACTERISTICS			
A. Enabling	Ability for Market-Work (Human Capital)			
1. good health		+	+	.020
2. preparation for work				
a. amount of formal schooling		+	+	.009
b. other training		+	+	.012
3. urban residence		+	+	.009
B. Precipitating	Necessity for Market-Work			
4. would work if unnecessary		–	+	.017
5. health limitations of husband		+	–	.005
6. income constraints				
a. income of husband		–	–	.030
b. number of dependents		+	–	.103
c. per capita family income		–	–	.031
C. Facilitating	Tastes for Market-Work			
7. age		+	0	
8. marital investment				
a. marital commitment		–	–	.090
b. age at first marriage		+	+	.047
c. number of marriages		+	+	.004
d. liberal attitude of husband		+	+	.243
e. education of husband		–	–	.013
9. Child investment				
a. number of children		–	–	.139
b. age first acquired children		+	+	.108
c. necessity of child care		–	+	.012
10. Subjective sex-role investment				
a. liberal attitude toward women working		+	+	.022
b. conservative attitude toward housekeeping		–	–	.003
c. conservative attitude toward child care		–	–	.013
11. Attitude toward job - like very much		+	+	.010
II. DEMAND	STRUCTURAL CHARACTERISTICS			
A. Job Conditions	Characteristics of the Job			
12. wages		+	+	.462
13. occupational grouping (unranked)***				.032
14. occupational sex-structure (% female)		–	–	.012
B. Marker Conditions (1971)	Environmental Characteristics			
15. demand for female labor		+	+	.010
16. area unemployment rates		–	0	
17. size of area labor force		+	+	.006

*conditions are measured circa 1967 with the exception for market conditions
**strength of the observed relation is indicated by the simple correlation ratio
***when occupations are ranked by "earnings," the ratio increases to 60 percent

REFERENCES

Agamau, T. and Maret, E.G. "Dimensions of Women's Labor Force Attachment." Paper presented at the annual meetings of the Southern Regional Demographic Group, Tallahassee, Florida, October 1980.

Bancroft, G. The American Labor Force. New York: John Wiley and Sons, 1958.

Bell, D. "Why Participation Rates of Black and White Wives Differ." Journal of Human Resources, Fall 1973, pp. 463-479.

Blau, P.M. and Duncan, O.D. The American Occupational Structure. New York: John Wiley and Sons, 1967.

Bowen, W.G. and Finegan, T.A. The Economics of Labor Force Participation. Princeton: Princeton University Press, 1969.

Buckley, J.E. "Pay Differences Between Men and Women in the Same Job." Monthly Labor Review 94 (1971): 36-39.

Cain, G.G. Married Women in the Labor Force. Chicago: The University of Chicago Press, 1966.

Chenoweth, L. and Maret-Havens, E. "Women's labor force participation--a look at some residential patterns." Monthly Labor Review 101 (1978): 38-41.

Cohen, M.S. "Sex Differences in Compensation." The Journal of Human Resources VI (4): 434-441.

Dahlstrom, E. The Changing Roles of Men and Women. Boston: Beacon Press, 1971.

Duncan, O.D. "A socioeconomic index for all occupations." In A.J. Reiss, et al., Occupations and Social Status. New York. Free Press, 1961.

Durand, J.D. The Labor Force in U.S.: 1890-1960. New York: Social Science Research Council, 1968.

Edwards, A. Comparative Occupation Statistics in the United States, 1870-1940. Washington, D.C.: U.S. Government Printing Office. 1943.

References (cont.)

Epstein, C.F. Woman's Place. Berkeley: University of California Press, 1970.

Falk, W.W. "Career development in theoretical perspective." In A.G. Cosby and I. Charner (ed.), Education and Work in Rural America: The Social Context of Early Career Decision and Achievement. Texas A&M University: Texas Agricultural Experiment Station. 1978.

Falk, W.W. and Cosby, A.G. "Women and the Status Attainment Process." Social Science Quarterly 56 (1975): 307-314.

Falk, W.W. "Women's Marital-Familial Statuses and Work Histories: Some Conceptual Consideration." Journal of Vocational Behavior 13 (1978): 126-140.

Ferriss, A.L. Indicators of Trends in the Status of American Women. New York: Russell Sage Foundation. 1971.

Featherman, D.L. and Hauser, R.M. "Sexual Inequalities and Socioeconomic Achievement in the U.S., 1962-1973." American Sociological Review 41 (1976): 462-483.

Fuchs, V.R. "Differences in Hourly Earnings Between Men and Women." Monthly Labor Review 94 (1971): 9-15.

Fuchs, V.R. "Hourly Earnings Differentials by Region and Size of City." Monthly Labor Review 90 (1967): 22-26.

Ginzberg, G. "Paycheck and Apron--Revolution in Woman Power." Industrial Relations 9 (1968): 193-203.

Gross, E. "Plus can change . . .? The Sexual Structure of Occupations Over Time." Social Problems 16 (1968): 198-208.

Havens, E.M. "Developing an Index to Measure Female Labor Force Attachment." Monthly Labor Review 100 (1977): 35-38.

References (cont.)

Havens, E.M. Women and the American Occupational
     Structure: (1) Women's Involvement in the Labor
     Force. Employment and Training Administration,
     U.S. Department of Labor. 1978.

Havens, E. and Gibbs, J.P. "The Relation Between
     Female Labor Force Participation and Fertility:
     A Theory of Variability." Sociological Methods
     and Research 3 (1975): 258-289.

Havens, E. and Tully, J.C. "Female Intergenerational
     Occupational Mobility: Comparisons of Patterns?"
     American Sociological Review 37 (1972): 774-777.

Hodge, R.W., Siegel, P.M., and Rossi, P.H.
     "Occupational Prestige in the United States,
     1925-63." American Journal of Sociology 70
     (1964): 286-302.

Horan, P.M. "Is Status Attainment Research
     Atheoretical?" American Sociological Review 43
     (1978): 534-541.

Knudsen, D.D. "The Declining Status of Women: Popular
     Myths and the Failure of Functionalist Thought."
     Social Forces 48 (1969): 183-193.

Knutson, M. and Schreiner, D. "Analysis of Factors
     Influencing Women's Labor Force Participation
     Decisions." Research Report P-723. Agricultural
     Experiment Station, Oklahoma State University,
     October 1975.

Mahoney, T.A. "Factors Determining the Labor Force
     Participation of Married Women." Industrial and
     Labor Relations Review 4 (1961): 563-577.

Mancke, R.B. "Lower Pay for Women: A Case for
     Economic Discrimination?" Industrial Relations
     10 (1971): 316-326.

Maret-Havens, E. "Developing an Index to Measure
     Female Labor Force Attachment." Monthly Labor
     Review 100 (1977): 35-38.

References (cont.)

Maret-Havens, E. and Gibbs, J.P. "The Relation Between
    Female Labor Force Participation and Fertility:
    A Theory of Variability." Sociological Methods
    and Research 3 (1975): 258-289.

Maret-Havens, E. and Tully, J.C. "Female
    Intergenerational Occupational Mobility:
    Comparisons of Patterns?" American Sociological
    Review 37 (1972): 774-777.

McClendon, M.J. "The Occupational Status Attainment
    Processes of Males and Females." American
    Sociological Review 41 (1976): 52-64.

McClendon, M.J. "Structural and Exchange Components of
    Vertical Mobility." American Sociological Review
    42 (1977): 56-74.

Mincer, J. "Labor Force Participation of Married
    Women: A Study of Labor Supply." In Aspects of
    Labor Economics. Princeton: Princeton
    University Press, 1962.

Morgan, J.N., et al. Income and Welfare in the United
    States. New York: McGraw-Hill, 1962.

National Manpower Council. Womanpower. New York:
    Columbia University Press, 1957.

National Manpower Council. Work in the Lives of
    Married Women. New York: Columbia University
    Press, 1958.

Nie, N., Bent, K.H., and Hu, C.H. Statistical Package
    for the Social Sciences. New York: McGraw-Hill,
    1970.

Oppenheimer, V.K. The Female Labor Force in the United
    States. Berkeley: Institute of International
    Studies, 1970.

Oppenheimer, V.K. "The Sex-Labeling of Jobs."
    Industrial Relations 7 (1968): 219-234.

Oppenheimer, V.K. The Female Labor Force in the United
    States. Berkeley: University of California,
    Population Monograph Series No. 5. (1970).

References (cont.)

Parnes, H.S. "Longitudinal Surveys: Prospects and Problems." Monthly Labor Review 95 (1972): 11-15.

Parnes, H.S., et al. Dual Careers: Volume I. Manpower Research Monograph No. 21, U.S. Department of Labor, Washington, D.C.: U.S. Government Printing Office, 1970.

Polachek, S.W. "Discontinuous Labor Force Participation and Its Effects on Women's Market Earnings." In Sex, Discrimination, and the Division of Labor, edited by C.B. Lloyd, pp. 90-122. New York: Columbia University Press, 1975.

Rogoff-Ramsøy, N. "Patterns of Female Intergenerational Occupational Mobility: A Comment." American Sociological Review 38 (1973): 806-807.

Rosenfeld, C. and Perrella, V.C. "Why Women Start and Stop Working: A Study in Mobility." (Special Labor Force Report No. 59) Monthly Labor Review, September 1965, pp. 1072-1082.

Rosenfeld, R.A. and Sorensen, A.B. "Sex Differences in Patterns of Career Mobility." Demography 16 (1979): 89-101.

Safilios-Rothchild, C. Women and Social Policy. Englewood Cliffs: Prentice-Hall, 1974.

Sanborn, H. "Pay Differences Between Men and Women." Industrial and Labor Relations Review 17 (1964): 534-550.

Sawhill, I.V. "The Economics of Discrimination Against Women: Some New Findings." Journal of Human Resources, Summer 1973, pp. 383-396.

Smuts, R.W. Women and Work in America. Schocken Edition. New York: Schocken Books, 1971.

Sobol, M.G. "Commitment to Work." In The Employed Mother in America. Edited by I. Nye and L.W. Hoffman. Chicago: Rand McNally, 1963.

References (cont.)

Sobol, M.G. "A Dynamic Analysis of Labor Force Participation of Married Women of Childbearing Age." Journal of Human Resources, Fall 1973, pp. 497-505.

Suter, L.E. and Miller, H.P. "Income Differences Between Men and Career Women." In Changing Women in a Changing Society, edited by J. Huber, pp. 200-212. Chicago: University of Chicago Press. 1973.

Sweet, J.A. "The Employment of Rural Farm Wives." Rural Sociology 37 (1972): 553-577.

Sweet, J.A. "Family Composition and the Labor Force Activity of American Wives." Demography, May 1970, pp. 195-209.

Sweet, J.A. Women in the Labor Force. New York: Seminar Press, 1973.

Treiman, D.J. and Terrell, K. "Women, Work, and Wages--Trends in the Female Occupational Structure Since 1940." In K.C. Land and S. Spilerman (ed.), Social Indicator Models. New York: Russell Sage Foundation. (1975).

The Twentieth Century Fund Task Force on Women and Employment. Exploitation from 9 to 5. Report of the Twentieth Century Fund Task Force on Women and Employment. Lexington, Massachusetts: Lexington Books. (1975).

Tyree, A. and Treas, J. "The Occupational and Marital Mobility of Women." American Sociological Review 39 (1974): 293-302.

U.S. Department of Labor, Dual Careers. Washington, D.C.: U.S. Government Printing Office, 1970.

U.S. Department of Labor, Fact Sheet on the Earnings Gap. Washington, D.C.: U.S. Government Printing Office, 1970.

U.S. Department of Labor, Bureau of Labor Statistics. Perspectives on Working Women: A Databook. Bulletin 2080. U.S. Government Printing Office. October 1980.

References (cont.)

Waite, L.J. "U.S. Women at Work." Population Bulletin 36 (May, 1981).

Waldman, E. "Women at Work: Changes in the Labor Force Activity of Women." Monthly Labor Review, June 1970, pp. 10-18.

Waldman, E. "Marital and Family Characteristics of the U.S. Labor Force." Monthly Labor Review, May 1970, pp. 18-27.

Weil, M.W. "An Analysis of Factors Influencing Married Women's Actual or Planned Work Participation." American Sociological Review, Fall 1961, pp. 91-96.

Weisskoff, F.B. "'Women's Place' in the Labor Market." American Economic Review 62 (1972): 161-166.

Williams, G. "A Research Note on Trends in Occupational Differentiation by Sex." Social Problems 22 (1975):543-547.

Williams, G. "The Changing U.S. Labor Force and Occupational Differentiation by Sex." Demography 16 (1979): 73-87.

Women's Bureau. 1969 Handbook on Women Workers. Washington, D.C.: U.S. Government Printing Office, 1969.

Women's Bureau. 1975 Handbook on Women Workers. Washington, D.C.: U.S. Government Printing Office, 1975.

Women's Bureau. "The Earnings Gap Between Women and Men." Washington, D.C.: U.S. Government Printing Office, 1979.

Zellner, H. "Discrimination Against Women, Occupational Segregation, and the Relative Wage." American Economic Review 62 (1972): 157-160.